*Leadership in the Library/Information Profession*

*Proceedings of the Twenty-sixth Annual
Symposium of the Graduate Alumni and Faculty
of The Rutgers School of Communication,
Information and Library Studies, 8 April 1988*

# Leadership in the Library/ Information Profession

*Edited by Alice Gertzog*

JANA VARLEJS, SERIES EDITOR

McFarland & Company, Inc., Publishers
*Jefferson, North Carolina, and London*

123579

This is the seventh in a McFarland series of Rutgers SCILS symposia under the general editorship of Jana Varlejs. The first six are *The Economics of Information* (1982), *The Right to Information* (1984), *Communication/Information/Libraries* (1985), *Freedom of Information and Youth* (1986), *Information Seeking* (1987), and *Information and Aging* (1988).

**British Library Cataloguing-in-Publication data available**


**Library of Congress Cataloguing-in-Publication Data**

*Leadership in the library/information profession* / edited by Alice Gertzog.
    p.  cm.
    Papers presented at the annual symposium of the graduate alumni and faculty of Rutgers School of Communication, Information, and Library Studies, April 9, 1988.
    Includes bibliographies.
    ISBN 0-89950-426-4 (sewn softcover; 55# acid-free natural paper) ∞
    1. Library administration — Congresses.  2. Information services — Administration — Congresses.  3. Leadership — Congresses.
I. Gertzog, Alice.  II. Rutgers University.  School of Communication, Information, and Library Studies.
Z678.L37   1989
025.1 — dc20
                        89-42716
                        CIP

© 1989 by the Rutgers Graduate School of Library and Information Studies Alumni Association

Manufactured in the United States of America.

*McFarland   Box 611   Jefferson NC 28640*

# Dedication

Thomas H. Mott, Jr., professor at Rutgers and dean of the Graduate School of Library and Information Studies from 1969 to 1983, died suddenly on January 18, 1989. He was a pioneer in introducing computer applications in library school curricula. He led the original Graduate School of Library Service as it evolved from a service oriented school grounded in the bibliographic tradition of librarianship through integration with the emerging discipline of information science into the new era of the multidisciplinary School of Communication, Information and Library Studies. Educated in mathematics and philosophy at Rice and Yale, he turned to the study of information processing and artificial intelligence in the 1950s. As dean of a library school, he synergized his interests in computers, books, management, and scholarship, and brought fresh vision to the challenge of preparing the library and information professionals of tomorrow. Under his leadership, the Rutgers GSLIS attracted stellar doctoral students who have assumed major responsibilities in libraries and professional education throughout the world. Under his leadership, a new kind of school for educating professionals for the Information Age has been created.

Because he was more a private than a public person, and perhaps fundamentally shy, Tom Mott will be remembered primarily for his achievements as a dean. However, those who were fortunate to know him well will remember him best as a scholar and a gentleman, and will miss him most for his warmth, zest, and generosity.

# Distinguished Alumni Award

The annual symposium of the graduate alumni faculty of Rutgers School of Communication, Information and Library Studies is generally an occasion for adding the name of a distinguished graduate to the roll of individuals who have brought honor to the School through their achievements. The 1988 Symposium followed this custom by honoring Professor Roger Greer for his service to the profession of librarianship. The citation presented to him on April 8 read as follows:

## TRIBUTE TO ROGER C. GREER

Whereas Roger C. Greer, who received his MLS from the Graduate School of Library Service in 1956 and Ph.D. from the Rutgers Graduate School in 1964 has brought national and international recognition to this university as a scholar, educator and researcher; and

Whereas he was an early and often cited contributor to empirical research in the areas of national and international book bibliography which assess characteristics, coverage and control; and

Whereas he was responsible for the design and implementation of a multi-methodological model of community analysis which has been used throughout the country, which included his founding of the Community Analysis Research Institute; and

Whereas he initiated an innovative doctoral program in information transfer and has more recently established a new model to integrate education and library information science and management and related disciplines at the undergraduate, masters, and doctoral levels which promises to be the basis for new fields and theories; and

Whereas he has served as library director, as dean of two accredited schools, as professor of two other universities and as currently professor and Dean Emeritus of the University of Southern California; and

Whereas his teaching both in and out of the classroom serves as a source of inspiration to others and it extends to his role of advisor and mentor to individuals who now serve our field as librarians, professors and deans; and

Whereas he has the rare combination of charm, charisma, sincerity and intelligence which makes him the role model for countless scores of librarians;

Be it therefore resolved that the Rutgers Graduate Alumni of the School of Communication, Information and Library Studies honors Roger C. Greer as the Distinguished Alumnus of the year 1988;

Be it further resolved that this distinction be spread upon the minutes of this Association and be made known to the library community.

# Acknowledgments

Thanks are due to Jeanette Walker, president of the Graduate Alumni of SCILS, Sally Wehr, who chaired the symposium committee, and Jan Glor, Rutgers Division of Alumni Relations liaison. Peggy Hoydis, as always, earns gratitude for her excellent work in transcribing the proceedings.

Joanne Euster's impressive performance in the moderator role kept the symposium on track and was much appreciated. Finally, thanks are due to the presenters, Joanne Euster, Emily Mobley and Robert Wedgeworth.

*Alice Gertzog*

# Table of Contents

# Introduction

## Alice Gertzog

The 1988 alumni-faculty symposium addressed a hot topic when it tackled "leadership." Presidential primaries and an impending national election had catapulted the discussion of leaders and leadership into the national consciousness. Talk about leadership permeated the atmosphere of the library world as well. Margaret Chisholm, then current president of the American Library Association, had designated 1987–88 as a year for stressing leadership development. Some six months prior to the symposium, Herb White in a *Library Journal* column had asked "Where Have All the Leaders Gone?" which became the pivotal question of the symposium. In addition, John Berry, editor of *Library Journal,* had written an editorial describing the new breed of public library leaders, and *New Jersey Libraries* had devoted an entire issue to concerns about leadership. A number of researchers were investigating aspects of library leadership from a variety of perspectives.

Although riding the coattails of a popular topic had not been the intent of the symposium planners, the fortunate confluence of national and professional concerns provided a subject of both timely and timeless interest to the diverse library community represented among the alumni and faculty who attended the April meeting. The symposium topic also served as an appropriate backdrop against which to honor Professor Roger Greer with the Distinguished Alumni Award for his lifelong attention to the leadership roles which libraries could and should play in their communities and the important leadership he himself has provided to the library/information community.

As a report on leadership, and particularly in librarianship, the symposium probably raised more questions for attendees than it answered. During the course of the wide-ranging presentations, speakers touched on many of the complex issues which have concerned leadership researchers and commentators over the centuries. While providing few unambiguous conclusions for the audience, the papers did serve to give listeners a heightened appreciation of the complexities involved in coming to grips with so difficult a concept as leadership.

The four papers represented four distinct approaches to the subject. Joanne Euster reviewed a typology of leadership styles evidenced by academic library directors. The typology was developed from research into how the perceptions about the behavior of library directors held by different constituencies of an academic community compared with self-assessments and with objective data regarding leader activities. Alice Gertzog, too, described a leadership research project, this one dealing with the qualities a group of "emergent leaders" of the library field were perceived as exhibiting, and, by inference, what librarians want or expect from library leaders. Bob Wedgeworth recounted the qualities he looks for in putative library leaders, placing special emphasis on "authority," "confidence," "ambition," "power" and "influence." Finally, Emily Mobley reported on the extent to which leadership positions in the library profession are currently held by members of minority groups and by women. She also described some of the barriers these two groups face in their efforts to achieve greater representation among the ranks of leaders.

Given the diverse approaches to the topic, it might be assumed that the papers presented here bear little relevance to each other. Yet, certain themes run through the talks and indicate similarities in the speakers' concerns and understanding about leadership. All of the participants described the elusive nature of the topic and the difficulties in defining it. Joanne Euster, quoting Mintzberg, pointed to the "you know" quality of leadership that makes us able to recognize, but not describe it. Alice Gertzog, adapting Kaufman and Jones' definition of power, suggested that leadership is "as abstract as time, yet as real as a firing squad." Three of the speakers referred to the tendency to equate management with leadership and stressed the importance of distinguishing between the two concepts.

All of the speakers noted the attention being focused on leadership, both in librarianship and in the greater society. Speculations about why the topic had achieved such national prominence centered on the perceived crisis in the production of political leaders and the greater emphasis on accountability. Similar fears about the production of library leaders, as well as the changing library environment, and uncertainties about the future of librarianship were offered as reasons for the increased attention to the topic in the library field. The situational context of leadership was acknowledged in other ways, as well. Mobley and Wedgeworth, for instance, both described events in their own lives which had presented leadership opportunities.

However, there was also an underlying assumption that leader traits are important and that studying how leaders behave is crucial to understanding leadership. Euster, for instance, examined the extent to which leaders were perceived as engaging in particular endeavors by administrators of universities as well as by the middle management of their libraries. Gertzog submitted a profile of traits which respondents to her survey associated with leadership. These traits included vision, assertiveness, and attention to professional concerns, among others. Mobley talked about the importance to leadership development of participation in professional organizations and Wedgeworth described a group of characteristics which he believed to be essential to leaders, and which he contended were probably developed early in life.

A spirited panel and audience discussion, much of which is reproduced here, addressed the crucial question of where the next generation of library leaders will come from. Wedgeworth and Gertzog contended that the leaders will arise to meet the profession's needs and will differ in where they come from by the arena in which they are required to provide leadership. Euster maintained that the term leadership needs to be redefined and that the library field ought to utilize what other fields have already learned about the subject. Members of the audience posed questions about the role of library schools in the production of leaders, whether certain personality types who are not leaders are attracted to the library profession, the difficulties in recruiting minorities to the field, and the schizophrenia which may result from minorities having to adapt to majority cultures and ways of behaving.

A final essay, "Thinking about Leadership," appears as an epilogue to these proceedings. In it, Gertzog reviews the overarching questions that have been associated with study of leadership and describes the theoretical positions held by some of those considered to be the foremost students of leadership.

# The Qualities of Leadership

*Joanne R. Euster*

It seems to me that recently libraries have been getting a big dose of conversation about leadership. It is not coincidental that a number of different individuals have chosen to focus on it at this time. American Library Association President Margaret Chisholm has taken as the theme for her presidential year, "Visionary Leaders for 2020." I recently completed and published a book, *The Academic Library Director: Management Activities and Effectiveness,* which, while dealing primarily with academic librarians, has information applicable to leaders of all kinds of libraries.

## Why Leadership Now?

Why is there so much discussion about leadership, or more appropriately, why is there so much discussion about the lack of leadership, right now, and in libraries? I think there are several answers. First, there is a perceived leadership crisis throughout the United States today. It is all pervasive. We are choosing political leaders on the basis of how they look, how they sound, and what we think their private lives tell us about their abilities to lead the country. We are afraid that we have lost our leadership position among the nations of the world, both politically and economically. You can't read a newspaper or a newsmagazine of any kind without finding an article on the subject. American business — what we used to refer to so smugly as "good old American know-how" — is now being blamed widely for much of our loss of economic leadership. You don't have to look very far to see this concern for leadership. It is even apparent on the best-seller list, in the real resurgence of biographies of people of accomplishment. Biography is one of the largest nonfiction best-seller categories right now. (Sometimes I think it's a fiction category as well, but that's another story.)

The second reason for the attention to leadership in libraries is the scrutiny and pressure for accountability that public agencies are experiencing. We are constantly hearing that private organizations can do a better job and that they can do it more cheaply. Higher education has come in for an unusual lot of criticism in recent years. Someone referred to the three B's, Bloom, Boyer, and Bennett, as being the people who constantly condemn American higher education. Allan Bloom's book, *The Closing of the American Mind,* had been on the *New York Times* Best Seller List for 45 weeks when I wrote this a few weeks ago. On that list it was exceeded only by Bernie Siegel's *Love, Medicine, and Miracles,* which had been on for 46 weeks. Considering that Bloom's book is practically unreadable, I think that's quite a record! The book's subtitle, *How Higher Education Has Failed Democracy and Impoverished the Souls of Today's Students,* probably pretty well summarizes what he has to say. It is a long, laborious lament about the loss of status of academics in American society. It's not a particularly good book, but it certainly has received a good deal of attention. Another of the B's, William Bennett, the secretary of education, is also constantly speaking about the failure of higher education. A rather influential book by Ernest Boyer, published by the Carnegie Commission the year before last, called *College, the Undergraduate Experience,* had a similar message.

## Library Leadership

Closer to home, that is to say in libraries, leadership has come in for a substantial amount of criticism, both recently and in the past. As far back as 1973, Charles Martell authored an article entitled: "Administration: Which Way—Traditional Practice or Modern Theory?" and concluded that library administration had fallen woefully behind in adopting changes in management theory from the behavioral and organization sciences. Shortly thereafter, Richard DeGennaro pointed out eloquently and forcefully that management theories were failures in practical application; that they did not correspond to experience or common sense, and they diverted attention from the real issues of administration. His conclusion was that management is an art, and not a science, and has to be practiced as such. Right after him came Charles McClure arguing that "academic library managers have not provided leadership in the solution of societal information problems, nor have they effectively utilized innovative managerial techniques to administer the library." In the immediate past, we have Herb White's *Library Journal* column, "Where Have All the Leaders Gone?" which was used as the headline on the announcement for this symposium.

So what has all this led to? Some of us went to business schools and earned MBA's. Some of us attended other kinds of management workshops, and brought home new learnings and experiences. Some of us have done a great deal of reading. Some of us who presumably had the needed skills and characteristics replaced library directors who retired or left their jobs for other reasons. In the meantime we go right on lamenting and searching for real leadership.

What does the research literature on management and leadership contain? Both concepts are heavily studied. However, leadership literature, inside and outside of libraries, is characterized by several significant gaps in understanding. The first is a tremendous confusion between the concepts of leadership and management. The second is a gap between the rather broad concept of leadership that is implied in the articles that describe the perceived shortage of leadership, and the quite narrow definitions that theorists and researchers are applying.

A look at the literature of leadership theory and research reveals a heavy focus on what sounds more like effective supervision than what most of us would call leadership. The critical writings are clearly asking for something more. They are seeking behaviors, I think, which will enable organizations to adjust to social and technological change, to develop meaningful goals, to design and implement the systems necessary to implement those goals, and to marshall the necessary resources.

When I began my research, I came to a few conclusions which became my underlying assumptions. First, adaptation to social and technological change is critical. Adaptation implies both an understanding of the environment external to the library and the ability of the library to draw resources for organizational change and survival from the environment. The second assumption is that adaptation implies very complex exchange relationships with the sources of funds and with those who determine policies and define regulations. The third basic assumption is that we are dealing with perceptions as well as realities.

In that framework, the objective of leadership is to infuse the organization with purpose and direction, to motivate members of the organization toward realization of organizational goals, and to influence positively the perceptions which the environment holds regarding the organization. This, in turn, permits the library to meet two goals: to create the output of goods and services that will meet patron needs, and to acquire the resources and social sanctions necessary for the library to expand and survive.

## The Two-Environment Model

In library language, what does this mean? Figure 1 is a model I developed to relate the role of the leader to the internal organization. It also relates the leader role to two aspects of the external environment. On the left side of the figure is the control environment, and on the right side the user environment. Most feedback models simply show outputs going out and feedbacks coming in with a single feedback loop. In this case I am suggesting a double loop because, on the one side, the "products" of our libraries are being used by individuals who don't have the decision-making power. The control environment, on the other hand, is the group that makes the decision about policies that govern the flow of resources to us. It is not necessarily the same body that is actually using our resources, our output.

This model is particularly descriptive of academic libraries, where the primary users are faculty and students and the decision makers are administrators, boards, legislatures, and so forth. In the middle is the library with the leader as intermediary between the control environment and the user environment as well as heading the internal organization that actually gets work done. From this position the leader is exerting influence toward the internal organization, affecting how it is organized and operated, and also exerting influence toward the control environment to affect the flow of resources and authority. The ability of the leader to effectively exert influence is related to the types of managerial and leadership activities in which he or she engages, but it is also related to the perceptions which the leader's two constituencies, members of the control environment and the internal organization, hold regarding the leader's and the library's effectiveness.

Within this framework, I conducted a study of academic library directors, to try to learn what they actually did to develop and maintain their influence role, how they were perceived by their constituencies, and what impact they had on their libraries.

I do not want to go into detail about the methodology I used for the study, but some background is essential. Most of the research was in the form of a survey which had several dimensions. A group of

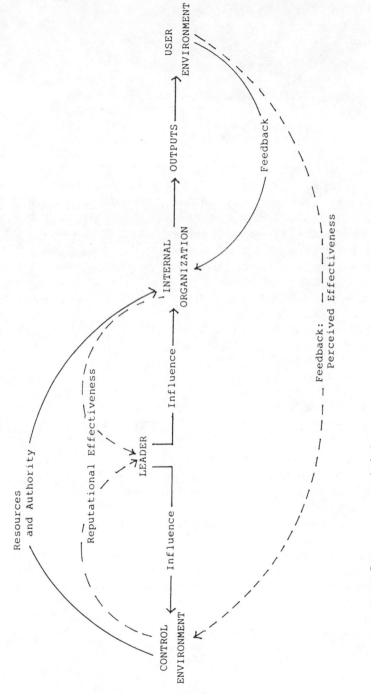

Resources
and Authority

Reputational Effectiveness

Influence

LEADER

Influence

CONTROL
ENVIRONMENT

USER
ENVIRONMENT

OUTPUTS

INTERNAL
ORGANIZATION

Influence

Feedback

Feedback:
Perceived Effectiveness

Resources, activities
Perceptions

# Leadership Roles

| Role | Focus |
|------|-------|
| Supervisor | I |
| Liaison | E |
| Environment Monitor | E & I |
| Entrepreneur | I |
| Spokesperson | E |
| Resource Allocator | E & I |

**Figure 2.**

academic library directors—distributed by size, by mix of public and private universities, and by geographical dispersion—were invited to participate in the study in advance of the survey being sent. To discover what managerial and leadership activities the directors performed, I used a 40-item questionnaire which had been developed from studies performed by Henry Mintzberg among top managers in business and industry. The library directors were asked to tell me the extent to which they engaged in these same activities. With their permission, I also sent the same instrument to two other groups in their colleges and universities—middle managers and dean-level colleagues—asking them to rate how well, or effectively the directors performed those tasks. I also asked directors to provide information on organizational changes that had occurred in the library in the last five years, and some demographic and professional information.

The questionnaire dealing with leader activities was cross-compared with the responses of the constituent groups. The managers reported how much effort they put into activities. The colleagues, in turn, described how effective managers were in performing those activities. Although they were not rating the same thing, they were using the same activity list and the same five-point rating scale.

Figure 2 groups the activities into six managerial roles: Supervisor, Liaison, Environment Monitor, Entrepreneur, Spokesperson and Resource Allocator. A focus is associated with each of these. The "I's" stand for "internally oriented" and the "E's" indicate "externally oriented," and describe whether the activities are related to the internal organization or toward the environment. In general, the directors

Opposite: Figure 1. The leadership role in the two-environment model (© 1986 Joanne R. Euster).

*Joanne R. Euster* 9

| Managerial Role | Managerial Activity Self-report | Effectiveness Ratings Mid Managers | Deans | Score Profiles 3   3.5   4   4.5 |
|---|---|---|---|---|
| Supervisor | 3.13 | 3.06 | 3.68 | |
| Liaison | 3.77 | 3.83 | 4.13 | |
| Environment Monitor | 3.68 | 3.68 | 4.07 | |
| Entrepreneur | 4.07 | 3.44 | 4.01 | |
| Spokesperson | 3.72 | 3.79 | 4.11 | |
| Resource Allocator | 3.84 | 3.48 | 3.87 | |
| Overall | 3.60 | 3.48 | 3.93 | |

Directors' report of extent of own activity
Mid Managers' ratings of managers' effectiveness
Deans' ratings of managers' effectiveness

**Figure 3. Mean scores for managerial roles (© 1986 Joanne R. Euster).**

expended the greatest effort in activities that were associated with the Entrepreneur role, followed by the Resource Allocator role. They expended the smallest amount of activity on the Supervisor role.

When leaders' estimates of activity were compared with the perception of effectiveness of middle managers and deans, some interesting divergences resulted which are displayed in Figure 3. Overall, the deans tended to rank the directors' effectiveness much higher than the middle managers, while, interestingly, the middle managers' perceptions of loose effectiveness were relatively congruent with the directors' assessment of their own effort. This led to two possible explanations. First, and most obvious, middle managers are in much better positions to observe directors' activities and to evaluate the results. Second, middle managers are simply more likely to know what goes on in a library. However, it may well be that deans are using a different framework for assessing the librarian, and are evaluating effectiveness more impressionistically and in terms of broad goals.

I also compared the rates of organization change with the amount of leader activity. The results are curious. Organization change might be assumed to be related to high levels of activity. However, only two kinds of change were found to be associated with high activity on the parts of the leaders. They were changes in facilities, and changes in the internal organizational structure. A very slight association was found with the introduction of revenue generating activities such as copy centers.

There have been studies in the past that suggested that innovation is positively related to organizational size. That is, that more change takes place in large organizations. I did not find that to be true in this case. Another popular supposition is that substantial change takes place under a newly hired library director because people are expecting immediate changes. As a matter of fact, for the 42 directors included in the study — 10 women and 32 men, a distribution which represents the population fairly well — there was a moderate association between brevity of their time in the job and the amount of change that had taken place.

The final relationship I looked at regarding organizational change had to do with the ability of the organization to adapt and keep up. One would expect that greater rates of change would correlate with higher effectiveness ratings for the director as a proxy for the effectiveness of the whole organization. In fact, results showed a moderate positive correlation in terms of changes in facilities, altered relationships with other university bodies, and in internal organizational changes, but the same positive correlation was not present in terms of the other activities.

## Leader Types

These general findings can be broken down more specifically. The three dimensions under discussion, again, are leader activity, organizational change and perceptions of effectiveness. On each of those three scales the directors were characterized as high or low. When there are three dimensions with two rankings, high and low, there are eight possible combinations. Figure 4 represents the distribution of those eight possible combinations among the 42 directors who were included in the study. There are four types that have a greater number of cases than would result from a random distribution of leader role activities, effectiveness ratings, and rates of organizational change. These four types were analyzed in more detail. Each of the four key types has been given a descriptive name:

• *Type 1,* which is high-activity, high-reputation and change is called *The Energizer.*

| Dimension | Leadership Type | | | | | | | |
|---|---|---|---|---|---|---|---|---|
| | I | II | III | IV | V | VI | VII | VIII |
| Reputational effectiveness | High N=29 | | | | Low N=13 | | | |
| Organizational change | High N=9 | | Low N=20 | | High N=3 | | Low N=10 | |
| Leader activity | High N=6 | Low N=3 | High N=9 | Low N=11 | High N=1 | Low N=2 | High N=3 | Low N=7 |
| | Energizer | | Sustainer | Politician | | | | Retiree |
| Code | HHH | HHL | HLH | HLL | LHH | LHL | LLH | LLL |
| Type | I | II | III | IV | V | VI | VII | VIII |

N=42

• *Type 3,* which is high-reputation and high-activity, but shows relatively little organizational change, I called *The Sustainer.*

• *Type 4,* also considered to be effective by colleagues and managers, shows low activity and very little organizational change and is termed *The Politician.*

• *Type 8* was named *The Retiree.* This indiviual exhibits little leader activity, receives low esteem from the community and runs an organization that doesn't experience much change.

The Energizer might be characterized as the leader of an excited or energetic organization. In terms of specific activities the Energizer devotes relatively more attention to the spokesperson role, which is externally focused, the entrepreneur role, which is internally focused, and the resource allocator role, which is both external and internal. Although for all the directors, supervisor activity was low, the Energizers' supervisor activity is higher within that low range—the highest of the lows. The Energizer, then, is someone who focuses activities both internally and externally, but with a slight emphasis on the internal organization, that is, on the library itself.

The Energizer's library is experiencing the greatest rate of change of any of the libraries included in the research. The greatest proportion of change in the Energizer's library is in the internal organization. The smallest amount of change is in facilities. However, Energizers have been in their jobs a very short time—typically only three and a half years, just a little more than half the time of the next shortest tenure type. It may be that the lack of change in facilities has to do with the long-term nature of planning and financing new or renovated facilities. Internal organizational changes are also consistent with the greater emphasis on leader activities that focus on the internal organization.

In terms of career patterns, Energizers suggest youth, energy and rapid career development. They can be either male or female; they are considerably younger than their colleagues—by about six years; they have occupied the greatest number of professional positions and have worked in the greatest number of individual libraries. Sixty-seven percent of them hold an advanced degree of some kind in addition to the MLS. Their professional involvement, interestingly, is rather low. On an index I had constructed to measure professional involvement, Energizers score about 25 percent lower than the population as a whole. This would be consistent with their emphasis on the internal organization. However, they tend to serve on somewhat more university

**Opposite: Figure 4. Eight leadership types (© 1986 Joanne R. Euster).**

committees than do their colleagues. It could be assumed that their external focus is close to home where it will have the greatest impact on the library. In summary, the Energizer is a leader who focuses on the organization and management of the library and who turns attention to outside arenas principally where they are seen as having an immediate impact on the library. The result is a rapidly changing library and high esteem for the leader.

The Sustainer has high reputational effectiveness and high leader activity, but relatively low change. These directors expend the most effort on liaison, entrepreneur and resource allocator activities. They also have a very high supervisor score relative to the total population. Thus they are fairly evenly focused internally and externally. Some of the greatest facilities changes have happened in libraries in this category. Sustainers have been in their positions a long time — over eight years. Since respondents were asked to report changes that had occurred within the last five years, it is conceivable that other changes took place earlier and were therefore excluded from consideration. The Sustainer's organization could by categorized as neutral or stable, experiencing relatively little change, but, at the same time, efficient with competent and comfortable leadership.

The Politician is characterized by low leader activity, low change in the library, and very high effectiveness ratings among the constituencies. Politicians accounted for 26 percent of the study population and fully one-third of the key types. For this reason, they are an important group. The size of this group would certainly contradict any assumption that high activity level, per se, results in high effectiveness ratings. Reputationally, Politicians resemble Energizers and Sustainers, but their total activity level is clearly the lowest of the four key types. They rank significantly low in supervisor, liaison, spokesperson roles and high only in entrepreneurial activities which do not result in high change.

There is one category of change in which Politicians scored high — higher than any other category — and that was in the area of automation. One might speculate that automation is a highly visible, desired innovation that affects reputation and, therefore, most likely to fit into this category. Careerwise, Politicians tend to be men, are about the norm in age, slightly below average in professional involvement, but very high in participation in university committees — the highest of all of the key types. This is particularly interesting because other research findings indicate that academic department membership in important university committees is positively related to high budget allocations. Although in many respects Politicians resemble Sustainers, they are really something of a puzzle. What distinguishes them is that Politicians have one outstanding characteristic that is different — visibility. They have chosen professional activities that bring them notice. The kinds of change they introduce are more visible and they are very selective about where they expend their efforts internally and externally.

Retirees form a significant group, 17 percent of the study population. They're characterized by limited leader activity; little experience of organizational change; and relatively low esteem by their colleagues, although low esteem may simply be a matter of being disregarded. This group does have some distinguishing characteristics. They are considerably older than their peers — the oldest group. Men and women are represented in about the same proportions as in the study as a whole. Retirees have been in their jobs the longest of any of the key types, nearly 12 years. They have worked in a fair number of libraries, but they have tended to occupy fewer total positions. Thus they have remained in individual jobs for longer time periods.

Retirees have the highest educational level of the entire population. Fifty-seven percent of them have doctorates, and 71 percent have advance degrees above the MLS. They differ, too, in terms of role activity. They tend to spend the greatest amount of effort in the resource allocator role and the least in supervisor and liaison roles. In terms of professional activities they read and scan professional journals and attend conferences at about the population mean, but much above the Energizer and the Politician. They participate in professional associations and attend continuing education workshops and courses at the highest level of any of the key types. Thus they are doing continuing education and learning experiences more than any other group. A few possibilities could account for this. One is that Retirees are not deeply involved in their libraries and seek professional stimulation and satisfaction elsewhere. Another equally valid possible explanation, however, and one that I would prefer, is that they sense an inadequacy and are attending professional meetings and continuing education in an effort to gather insights and information that will bring them back into the mainstream.

There is one more factor about Retirees which merits attention. In terms of university committee assignment, one would expect a person with elder statesman status in a college or university to be heavily used for university committees. This is not the case. Retirees score significantly low on university committee assignments.

Based on this data, it can be concluded that there really is no single factor, or even a pair of factors, that could be conclusively related to a third. What emerges is a variety of leadership types. Three of the four

*Joanne R. Euster*   15

key types had high reputations inside and outside their libraries. They made up 62 percent of the total study population. Everything else about them was different. They engaged in a variety of activities and approached their jobs in different ways. This, I think, is an expression of the idiosyncratic nature of leadership and why, if you read the literature, leadership has shown itself to be fairly resistant to analysis. It is also an expression of organizational difference and the degree of fit that is needed between the library and the leader's style. Organizational culture changes. Organizations' needs for structure and for stability appear to be cyclical. Furthermore, leader behavior is constrained and to some extent directed by beliefs about what is and what is not appropriate activity for the organization to engage in, and by the expectations that constituents have for the organization. Within this framework, the variety of leader types who were rated as being effective in their work would reflect the degree to which the director's management behaviors were congruent with the needs and expectations of the university and the library.

## Studying Leadership

At this point, I want to leave my own study and come back to the larger issue. There has been a painful gap between what I call the quest for leadership and the study of it by organizational and behavioral theorists who seem to feel that if they dissect a flower into small enough parts they will discover the secret of beauty. My research is in their tradition, but moves away from it in the attempt to integrate both reality and common sense into a systematic study of leadership.

The books of two leadership theorists who bring a practical and applicable vision to leadership study should be mentioned here. The first is *Leaders: The Strategies for Taking Charge,* by Warren Bennis and Burt Nanus. Bennis is a former college president and now a professor of management at the University of Southern California. Bennis and Nanus speak about "transforming leadership," a term coined by James MacGregor Burns in his book *Leadership.* They see the true leader as pursuing four behavioral strategies: 1) having a clear vision of the organization; 2) communicating that vision so that it defines reality for the group; 3) developing trust among followers by choosing a direction and then persevering with it; and 4) having the self-respect and self-knowledge to engender self-confidence in others.

The second book is by Harlan Cleveland and is called *The Knowledge Executive: Leadership in an Information Society.* Cleveland has had a long career in government service as well as in academics. He was, for a time, United States ambassador to NATO, and has been president of the University of Hawaii and dean of the Hubert Humphrey Institute of Public Affairs at the University of Minnesota where, though no longer dean, he remains on the faculty. Cleveland's vision is one of an information society so complex and so interdependent that no one person can be in charge of an organization—truly in charge. He refers to the "nobody in charge society." Yet he leaves the reader with hope. If the skills and knowledge of all members of the organization are used to provide information and understanding, the organization can run well. The role of the leader is to be a generalist. The leader cannot be a specialist for there is simply far too much to know. The leader needs to be a member of what Cleveland calls the "get it all together profession." This is the salvation for the "nobody in charge society." This is the person or group of people who bring vision, communication and coordination to the organization. They supply the form and process.

I would like to close with a quote from Mintzberg: "We are unable to define it, but we sure seem to know it when we see it," he said of leadership. Bennis and Nanus put it another way: "Like love, leadership is something everybody knew existed, but nobody could define."

# References

Bennis, Warren G., and Burt Nanus. *Leaders: The Strategies for Taking Charge.* New York: Harper and Row, 1985.

Bloom, Allan. *The Closing of the American Mind.* New York: Simon and Schuster, 1987.

Boyer, Ernest. *College, the Undergraduate Experience.* New York: Harper and Row, 1987.

Cleveland, Harlan. *The Knowledge Executive.* New York: Truman Talley Books/E.P. Dutton, 1985.

DeGennaro, Richard. "Library Administration and New Management Systems." *Library Journal* (December 15, 1978): 2477–2482.

Euster, Joanne R. *The Academic Library Director. Management Activities and Effectiveness.* New York: Greenwood, 1987.

McClure, Charles R. "Library Managers: Can They Manage? Will They Lead?" *Library Journal* (November 15, 1979): 2388–2391.

Martell, Charles. "Administration: Which Way—Traditional Practice or Modern Theory?" *College and Research Libraries* 33(1972): 104–112.

Mintzberg, Henry. *The Nature of Managerial Work.* New York: Harper and Row, 1973.

White, Herbert. "Oh, Where Have All the Leaders Gone?" *Library Journal* 112 (October, 1987): 68–69.

# Perceptions of Leadership

*Alice Gertzog*

I approached the study of leadership in a different context from the one Joanne Euster used to investigate the academic library leaders. I looked at the leadership of an applied field rather than that of a scholarly discipline, on the one hand, or the leadership of a formal organization, on the other. Therefore I did not assume, as one might when investigating a scholarly field, that research prowess and leadership are synonymous.

Nor did I assume, as studies of those formal organizations might, that "headship," that is, titular leadership, is synonymous or coincident with "emergent" leadership, although I recognized the possibility that often they would be. The prime difference that I saw between "headship" and "leadership" is a function of the source of the power to influence. In a formal organization with appointed heads, the authority has its source outside the group. In a public library, for instance, a board appoints the head librarian. In an academic institution, the university or college is responsible for appointing a library director. In a voluntary organization, however, it is the group itself that confers authority.

The topic seemed important to investigate because leadership affects change. It may further it. It may impede it, but it is certainly instrumental in its effect on change. Therefore, leadership is crucial to agenda-setting. Where we are going in the future has to do with who are our leaders and what they represent.

I set out to identify, through some surveys, a group of perceived current American library leaders in order to answer a number of research questions. What I want to stress is that the list I identified and used does not represent a definitive list of library leaders. It is merely *a* list of names of those perceived by a particular survey universe as providing leadership to the library field today.

# Research Questions

Four broad research areas were addressed during the course of my investigation. They included the *locus* of leadership, the extent of *connectedness* or *integration* within the field, the degree to which there is a shared *definition* of leadership, and attention to the *background* and *activities* of those named as field-wide leaders. The following is a list of questions, broken down by the above areas, which were investigated:

First, what does a list of perceived leaders of the library community reveal about the social structure of the library world? In other words, what do the institutional identifications of leaders reveal about the structure of the field? Is the leadership coming only from academic librarians; from only one subfield? To what extent do gender and geography seem to be reflected in the perception of leadership?

Secondly, to what extent can the library profession be considered integrated or connected? To what extent are the same people identified as leaders across subfields? To what extent do members of various subfields agree on where leadership is coming from?

A third group of questions had to do with the definition of leadership. When presented with a group of reasons, do people select the same ones to explain their choices of leaders? This is the subject I am going to treat today.

The final group of questions dealt with whether those identified as leaders of the library profession share backgrounds and characteristics. Have all leaders studied at Yale? Were they raised in the Northeast? Do they write for library periodicals? If so, which kind? Is activity in ALA synonymous with leadership?

These are questions that were addressed in my research.

This study dealt with the *perception* of leadership. But are those who we perceive to be leaders really leaders? Is there such a thing as a *real* leader? The investigation was based on the premise that a person who is identified as a leader fits definitionally into someone's understanding of a leader. Therefore, for purposes of this study, any person named as a leader is considered one. Some comments which accompanied the returned questionnaire suggested skepticism on the part of respondents about this approach to the identification of leaders. "Oh, that's a popularity poll," one man wrote. I contend, however, that for these purposes, popularity is an important aspect of leadership.

How a society defines leadership at any given time will produce different leader-name lists. For instance, if we see leadership as the contribution of a specific idea or of a technology, the names that emerge are likely to be the Edisons, Bells and Fords. On the other hand, if we talk about action and/or persuasion, the names may be the Roosevelts, Wilsons or Hearsts. Even with mutually acceptable operational definitions, leadership may be observer-dependent and a product of such factors as selective perception, cognitive dissonance and other psychological elements. On the other hand, who a society names as its leaders gives strong indication of that society's values at a moment in time. Actors and sports heroes as leaders reflect the values or priorities of a community vastly different from one which reveres philosophers and poets.

## Methodology

In order to compile a list of perceived leaders, I administered two surveys. The first one, Figure 1, asked respondents—a group of about 600 library connected persons—to name up to 15 people who "you think are providing the greatest leadership in the library field today, and to indicate why you have chosen the names you are submitting." A list of reasons, described below, for selecting leaders was provided. Consider for a minute how you might have reacted had you received this questionnaire in the mail—some of you probably did. If you were not fed up with all the questionnaires which had recently appeared in your mailbox, how might you have responded to this question?

For some of you, finding enough names to fill out the questionnaire would present a very difficult challenge, particularly if your orientation is not toward the field as a whole, but rather toward your own subfield, or perhaps even toward your own institution. On the other hand, those of you who may be part of the wider library world—its communication media, its organizations, and so on—might have difficulty limiting yourselves to 15 names.

Based on the nominations I received, a second questionnaire was constructed which listed the 101 leaders who were most frequently named in responses to the first survey. The second survey was also distributed to about 600 members of the library community. Each was asked to check the names of no more than 15 of the listed nominees who they perceived to be providing the greatest leadership to the field, and to circle reasons for their selections. The rate of response to the second questionnaire was much heavier than the rate had been for the first survey. When provided with a list of names, people apparently found choosing among them relatively simple. The task of supplying names, on the other hand, may have seemed far more challenging.

The list of most frequently named leaders from both surveys was utilized to draw up a list of 16 "Field-Wide" leaders. The list of leaders called "field-wide" represented those whose nominations or selections had been both broad-based across subfields and frequent.

The questionnaires were color-coded to indicate the type of librarianship with which respondents were currently associated. Library educators, for instance, received yellow forms and academic librarians were sent green ones. This method made it possible to cross-tabulate the results to learn whether nominators were selecting members of their own subfields. In the same way, inclusion of a few biographical questions about respondents' gender and current geographic location could also be utilized to look at relationships. For instance, the extent to which women named women, or Easterners cited their regional compatriots could be tracked.

## Survey Universe

The universe of respondents to whom the surveys were mailed included:

Directors of *public* libraries with annual budgets of more than $1 million;

Directors of *academic* libraries with collections of at least one-half million titles;

Directors of *special* libraries with at least six professional employees;

*Library Educators* above the rank of assistant professor and including emeriti professors;

*School Librarians* whose districts encompassed the largest number of school libraries and media centers;

A category labeled *Other,* which included all state librarians, administrators of library organizations, consortia directors, heads of library publications including scholarly and popular journals, publishers of library-related books, and the directors of two agencies whose libraries did not seem to fit into any of the other categories — the New York Public Library and the Library of Congress.

The views of this group, rather than a random sample of the profession, were sought for a number of reasons. These librarians probably have been in the profession longer. Librarians in higher positions are more apt to be involved in what systems theorists describe as

THE STATE UNIVERSITY OF NEW JERSEY

# RUTGERS

Please name up to fifteen people who you think provide the greatest leadership in the library field. (Do not feel compelled to produce 15 names. That number has been suggested only as an upper limit.) Categories of possible reasons for nominations follow the space for your selection. Circle all those which you feel apply. Feel free to provide additional reasons which influenced your selections. Please complete the three short items at the end of the questionnaire.

Name:

| Prof.Organization Participation | Institutional Position | Innovations | Research/ Writing | Contribution of Ideas | Personal Characteristics | Other |

Comments:

Name:

| Prof.Organization Participation | Institutional Position | Innovations | Research/ Writing | Contribution of Ideas | Personal Characteristics | Other |

Comments:

Name: _____

| Prof.Organization Participation | Institutional Position | Innovations | Research/Writing | Contribution of Ideas | Personal Characteristics | Other |
|---|---|---|---|---|---|---|
| | | | | | | |

Comments:

Name: _____

| Prof.Organization Participation | Institutional Position | Innovations | Research/Writing | Contribution of Ideas | Personal Characteristics | Other |
|---|---|---|---|---|---|---|
| | | | | | | |

Comments:

Please complete the following:
1. Gender: Male ( )  Female ( ); 2. If you have an MLS degree, year earned: 19___;
3. State in which you are currently located:

Figure 1. Survey used to determine who provides the greatest leadership in the library field.

boundary-spanning activities. They bear the heaviest financial and other professional responsibilities and are the ones most directly and immediately affected by leadership in the field. Most librarians, like workers in other professions, devote only a fraction of energy to matters of diagnosis, innovation, deliberate change and growth. Day-to-day concerns occupy their time. They are involved in routine, goal-directed activities and don't have time to think about leadership. Finally, innovations usually enter a hierarchical system at the top through individuals who are of relatively higher socioeconomic status.

There are certain drawbacks, of course, to administering a questionnaire in this particular fashion. Six subfields do not adequately describe the library profession. Rural public librarians in systems do not have much in common with urban public librarians. Community college librarians do different work than those in large university libraries. Special libraries are so diverse that they can hardly be called a group. For purposes of this research, however, the divisions seemed adequate.

One group presented a real problem, and did so almost from the outset of the research. The intention had been to draw up a list of school/media librarians who collectively were commensurate to groups of survey recipients in the other subfields — those who are responsible for the largest organizations within their subfields. There seemed, however, to be no source that would provide the information needed to construct such a group. School librarians and library educators from all over the country were contacted, as were consultants at the United States Office of Education. No one could point to a list or suggest a direction. Finally, a *sample* of school librarians was devised. But it is a less than satisfactory list. My inability to identify an appropriate cohort of school librarians may have been the first important finding of this research.

## Defining Leadership

Today I want to share with you some insights into what some titular leaders of the library field seem to want or to find in their emergent leaders. No definition of leadership accompanied the questionnaire for either survey. Meaning was assumed to be individual and to reside in respondents. An analysis of their nominations and their reasons for naming people as leaders would be used to decide whether, and, if so, which definitions were broadly shared by the library community.

This lack of definition was recognized with complaint by five or six respondents. The vast majority of survey recipients, however, did not object. They were perfectly content just to fill out the questionnaire without a definition. To them, "leadership" was simply a word, a concept, whose definition is self-evident.

Herb Kaufman and Victor Jones, two political scientists, explain how "power," a concept not unrelated to leadership, is also difficult to define, yet broadly understood:

> There is an elusiveness about power that endows it with an almost ghostly quality. It seems to be all around us, yet this is "sensed" with some sixth sense. We "know" what it is, yet we encounter endless difficulties in trying to define it. We can "tell" whether one person or group is more powerful than another, yet we cannot measure power. It is as abstract as time, yet as real as a firing squad.[1]

The reasons given by respondents to explain their selection of leaders provides a foundation for inferring the qualities of leaders in the library profession.

Verbal statements volunteered by respondents to amplify or explain their choices were analyzed to determine whether they corroborate the selection of reasons from the choices provided or whether they reveal latent meanings not apparent in the ostensible choices.

## Findings

On the first questionnaires appeared a list of six categories of reasons that were suggested to respondents. They were:

- "Professional organization participation,"
- "Institutional position,"
- "Innovations,"
- "Research/writing,"
- "Contribution of ideas,"
- "Personality."

A pilot study had produced 43 reasons for selecting leaders. The categories utilized emerged from those reasons. Respondents, of course, had the option to supply additional reasons, and space was provided for that purpose, although not many availed themselves of that opportunity.

The categories of reasons form a rough continuum from objective—"Professional organization participation" and "Institutional position"— to subjective—"Personal characteristics." The typology also represents, in its polarities, choices which lead, on the one hand, to a description of leadership as "situation" ("institutional position"), to leadership by virtue of individual traits ("personal characteristics"), on the other. Together they address the age-old question: Is situation or trait responsible for leadership? Do circumstances create leaders, or do leaders create circumstances propitious for exercising leadership?

Respondents were not limited to one or two reasons. If they so chose, they could circle all of the reasons. Failure by a respondent to select a particular reason did not necessarily indicate a negative decision — that the nominee did not exhibit that attribute. It only implied that the reason or reasons were less compelling.

"Contribution of ideas" was identified as the most important reason for selecting nominees. More than 70 percent of the respondents to the first survey cited it. Responses to the second survey did not reveal as heavy a concentration of votes for that category, but it remained the most frequently selected reason for naming leaders, and was chosen by half of this latter group.

"Institutional position" was offered as a reason for selecting a nominee by 54 percent of all those who replied to the first survey.

At the other extreme, "Personal characteristics" and "Innovations" emerged as the least selected reasons for naming people as leaders in the case of both surveys.

Slight variations in choices of reasons appear when responses are divided by subfields. For instance, although a majority of respondents from five of the subfields selected "Contribution of ideas" as the most important reason, library educators placed it second, according first rank to "Institutional position" by a two percentage point margin (66 percent to 64 percent). However, few *major* substantive variations in reasons for choosing leaders emerged in the findings.

Gender, too, was examined to learn whether it is a factor that influenced the choice of reasons for selecting leaders. The findings indicated that women and men behaved similarly with only a few minor differences.

Those participating in the surveys generally agreed on the reasons why they name the leaders. Further, I think it can be inferred that characteristics they identified leaders as exhibiting are the ones that they desire in leaders. In other words, most of the respondents to these questionnaires named leaders because they "contribute ideas" and I think we can infer that they want leaders who provide this quality. They also perceive that leaders must have a position from which to advance those ideas. Respondents considered the contribution of "innovations" and "personality" of lesser importance.

# Volunteered Comments

Eighty-six respondents to the first survey and 14 respondents to the second volunteered comments, sometimes at great length, to explain their nominations. When respondents used their own words to articulate leadership qualities, in addition to responding with a checkmark or a circle to a group of preselected attributes, subtle patterns of response begin to appear that add dimension to the definition of leadership.

Respondents' comments fell into three categories. One set of remarks implied that leaders were "problem solvers" and mentioned specific activities of nominees. Under this heading might fall such comments as: "for her work with the continuing library education network," or "efforts for adult literacy." A second group described the characteristics and roles played by nominees, as in "mover and shaker" or "perfect mentor." These implied "leader as person." And a third group identifies leaders merely by institution, such as John Doe, N. Y. Public Library. This category might be called "leader as position holder."

Respondents had placed "innovation" among the least important reasons why leaders were chosen. Yet, in the written responses, substantial numbers of comments, particularly those which describe "leader as problem solver," stressed its importance. Correspondents regularly alluded to innovation, occasionally utilizing the term itself, sometimes employing synonyms. On occasion the word "innovation" was not checked despite an accompanying description which clearly marked a nominee as an innovator. Following is a sample of some of the words that people used to describe innovators as leaders: "pioneer," "initiator," "developer," "inventor," "promoter," and "architect."

Accompanying these nominal descriptions were the fields in which innovators are doing their work. They include: 1)technological interests, such as automation, information systems; 2) library interest such as bibliographic instruction; and 3) social concerns such as intellectual freedom, the homeless, information access, and so on.

A partial explanation of this contradiction between what respondents checked on their questionnaires and the thrust of their comments can be found in the problem of definition described above. "Contribution of ideas" and "Innovations" are not mutually exclusive categories. Rather, they are related. The distinctions between them are unclear. Respondents seemed to interpret "Innovation" as referring more to specific technological advances and new methods than to general concepts or ideas. Therefore "vision" and similar terms are likely to be ascribed to those who "Contribute ideas" rather than to "Innovators."

| Gertzog — Written Comments | | | Stogdill — Positive Research Findings | | |
|---|---|---|---|---|---|
| A. Personality | 156 | (51%) | A. Personality | 162 | (46%) |
| activist | 37 | (12%) | aggressiveness | 12 | ( 3%) |
| controversial | 23 | ( 8%) | ascendance/ dominance | 31 | ( 9%) |
| | | | alertness | 4 | ( 1%) |
| | | | enthusiasm | 3 | ( 1%) |
| | | | extroversion | 1 | ( 1%) |
| | | | objectivity | 7 | ( 2%) |
| vision | 27 | ( 9%) | originality/ creative | 13 | ( 4%) |
| movers | 15 | ( 3%) | resourcefulness | 7 | ( 2%) |
| innovators | 13 | ( 4%) | | | |
| reasonable | 11 | ( 4%) | adjustment | 11 | ( 3%) |
| dignity | 6 | ( 6%) | emotional balance | 14 | ( 4%) |
| | | | self-confidence | 28 | ( 8%) |
| | | | tolerance of stress | 9 | ( 3%) |
| inspiring | 14 | ( 5%) | ------- | | |
| ------- | | | personal integrity | 9 | ( 3%) |
| personality | 10 | ( 3%) | ------- | | |
| B. Social Chars. | 68 | (22%) | B. Social Chars. | 81 | (23%) |
| administrative | 27 | ( 9%) | administrative | 16 | ( 5%) |
| concerned | 15 | ( 3%) | nurturance | 4 | ( 1%) |
| educator | 11 | ( 4%) | tact/diplomacy | 4 | ( 1%) |
| political | 13 | ( 4%) | abil. to enlist coop. | 3 | ( 1%) |
| admired | 6 | ( 2%) | popularity/ prestige | 1 | ( -%) |
| | | | sociability | 35 | (10%) |
| | | | social participation | 9 | ( 3%) |
| | | | cooperativeness | 5 | ( 1%) |
| | | | attractiveness | 4 | ( 1%) |
| C. Task Related Characteristics | 41 | (13%) | C. Task Related Characteristics | 54 | (15%) |
| conscientious | 11 | ( 4%) | responsible | 6 | ( 2%) |
| professionalism | 10 | ( 2%) | drive for responsib. | 17 | ( 5%) |
| scholar | 5 | ( 2%) | task orientation | 13 | ( 4%) |
| gatekeeper | 5 | ( 2%) | | | |
| consultant | 4 | ( 1%) | | | |
| entrepreneur | 6 | ( 2%) | enterprise | 10 | ( 3%) |
| | | | achievement | 21 | ( 6%) |
| D. Intelligence and Ability | 40 | (13%) | D. Intelligence and Ability | 58 | (16%) |
| fluency of speech and writing | 23 | ( 8%) | fluency of speech | 15 | ( 4%) |
| intelligence | 15 | ( 3%) | intelligence | 25 | ( 7%) |
| knowledge | 2 | ( 1%) | knowledge | 12 | ( 3%) |
| | | | judgment/ decisiveness | 6 | ( 2%) |
| Totals | 305 | | | 355 | |

Interestingly, lack of regard for "innovators" is not uncommon. Studies have found that often the most innovative members of a system are seen as deviating from the norms of the social system and are accorded somewhat dubious status and low credibility by average members of the system. Change agents, on the other hand, and opinion leaders, enjoy higher status and more respect.[2]

"Ideas" for these library respondents seemed to occupy a higher rung than did "Innovations."

Similar blurring occurred in the overlap between "Ideas" and "Research/writing," and between "Research/writing" and "Innovations." In another, and probably the most interesting apparent contradiction, "Personal characteristics" was chosen as the leadership factor fewer times than any other reason with the exception of "Innovation." Yet most of the volunteered statements about leaders revealed a concern for "Personal characteristics" of nominees.

In an effort to resolve this contradiction, a classification system developed by Stogdill was adopted and used to categorize and interpret respondent comments that were classified under "Leader as person." Figure 2 shows the four Stogdill categories utilized. It reports the number of mentions by respondents to these surveys, and compares them with the number of positive research findings reported by Stogdill.

The traits are divided into umbrella categories which differentiate leader characteristics associated with individual abilities (Intelligence and Ability); essential character (Personality); the approach to tasks (Task-Related Characteristics); and relations with other people (Social Characteristics).

Most written comments made in conjunction with this study were associated with "Personality" characteristics. More than half of the total remarks under the rubric "Leader as Person" can be classified within that category. "Social Characteristics" ranked second. Fewer comments were associated with traits which are "Task-Related" or with those which concerned "Intelligence and Ability."

Some factors contributing to the large number of comments applied to "Personality" characteristics may be present in recent revisionist thinking about the contribution of personality and personal traits to leadership. At the beginning of the century, and certainly before that, there was a strong belief that leaders were superior people and that personality was largely responsible for leadership. By the middle of the

**Opposite: Figure 2. Characteristics of leaders (adapted from Stogdill, 1981, p.76).[3]**

century, the situationists held sway and personality was believed to be of little consequence.

Contemporary researchers stand on a middle ground and have come to believe that personality is an important factor in leadership differentiation. There has not been a total return to the trait approach. Currently, the conventional view holds that some of the variance in who emerges as a leader is due to traits required by situation.

Following is a summary of the volunteered comments that respondents contributed regarding their leader nominations:

Under Personality there are five groups of related traits which dominate not only the personality category, but the entire range of written comments. Together they account for almost three-quarters of the comments in the personality category and nearly 40 percent of the total characteristics implicit in the comments of all survey recipients. The five groups are "activity," "controversy," "vision," "innovation," and "movement." The linkage among these terms is signaled, for me, by a shared impression of motion, force and advancement.

Many of the words subsumed under "activist" or "controversial" connote combat. They are strident in tone, and carry a hint of frustration and anger. Respondents used words such as "challenging," or "cuts red tape," "ruthless," "strong," "tough," "pulls no punches," and "seizes timely issues" to describe leaders. Words classified in the categories of "activist" and "controversial" suggest that library field members who responded to these questionnaires value leaders who are willing to speak up for library issues and for librarians.

The high regard accorded leaders with "vision" and the two related subdivisions, "innovators" and "movers," may reflect a community, as one correspondent wrote, "very much in parenthesis." The words "vision" and "visionary" appear in ten comments, "creative" appears in five and the notion of "foresight" and "future" in at least five more. Insecurity about how change will be manifested may prompt a desire for leaders who are perceived as able to influence the direction of change.

Under Social Characteristics, people-oriented skills, particularly those which can be called "administrative," were mentioned frequently in comments about library leaders. Joanne Euster has written elsewhere that "library literature, like management literature in general, has tended to confuse the modern techniques of effective administration with leadership." Comments about "administrative ability," "good management techniques," "supervision," are manifestations of this confusion.

Fewer comments appeared under "educator" than I had anticipated. After all, most respondents had attended library school.

Almost a third of the survey universe were themselves currently library educators. Researchers who have studied innovation ascribe substantial importance to the role of the university in leadership. I had anticipated, therefore, that the concept of teaching or mentoring would draw more than the 11 comments classified under "educator." The lack of comment regarding education may be evidence that respondents were more likely to think of leadership in terms of policy or pragmatic considerations than in terms of the transmission of theoretical or intellectual matters.

Under Task-Related Characteristics, "professional orientation" itself drew ten comments. Statements described leader efforts in behalf of professional "standards," "values," and "image," and they seemed to buttress the contention that at least some of those identified as library field leaders are perceived as exhibiting a willingness to vigorously support the profession.

The concept of "scholar" received only five mentions. Perhaps the activities associated with scholarship are subsumed under other categories, such as Intelligence and Ability, where such terms as "thinking" and "writing" appear. The lack of reference to scholarly endeavor may corroborate my assumption that respondents viewed leadership in terms of "policy" considerations rather than "academic" ones. I was surprised to find that activities related to agenda-setting, agenda-controlling, or other aspects of the "gatekeeping" function, all of which can be considered policy oriented, also received scant attention in comments from respondents. "Gatekeeping" is an activity associated with power, and power as "control" is another characteristic not mentioned in comments.

Finally, comments associated with "fluency of speech and writing" ranked highest among the characteristics associated with "Intelligence and Ability." Both written and oral "eloquence" were stressed in 23 comments alluding to communication skills.

Fifteen respondents referred to the "intelligence" of the leaders they nominated, but they seemed to be identifying "clarity of thought" rather than "intellectuality."

Library respondents did not comment about leaders' "knowledge." Only two statements could be classified under that heading. Perhaps we assume our leaders will be knowledgeable, and therefore we consider it unnecessary to mention that characteristic.

Those who define leaders simplistically as "people who help to guide or direct," provide little insight into distinctions that might be made among individual leaders or into distinctions about how leaders differ in terms of the culture they serve.

Fortunately, the data available from the words and phrases used by members of the library field to describe their leaders further this research in two important ways:

1) They lend subtlety and dimension to the broad concepts represented by attributes on the checklist of reasons. It is assumed that traits which are frequently mentioned have importance. Conversely, those which have received no mention are of less consequence to respondents either because they are expected to be present and therefore need not be mentioned, or because they are not germane to the question posed; and

2) The data permit comparisons about the traits required or perceived as exhibited by library field members and the traits which might be needed by members of formal organizations or academic disciplines.

## Summary

To summarize: Written comments characterize leaders in order of frequency of mention as activist, with vision, controversial, fluent in speech and writing, and as having administrative skills. Traits which describe individual psychology, particularly in terms of motivation and power, are absent. Also relatively less often cited are the amount of intelligence, knowledge, or scholarly endeavor which leaders exhibit. Teaching is mentioned to a moderate degree.

The words and phrases used to describe leadership in a more academic discipline might include scholarship, contribution to the theoretical and conceptual framework of a subject, judicious consideration of evidence, and authority predicated on knowledge.

The terms used to characterize leadership in a formal organization might include, in addition to a heavy emphasis on administrative skills, sociability and an orientation toward mobilizing energy toward a specific task, two types of skills which received infrequent comments by library field members.

Responding to a set of preselected reasons for naming people as leaders, survey participants generally agreed that the "contribution of ideas" was of primary importance, and that, secondarily, the "institutional position" occupied by the nominee was also salient. Of much less importance were "Personal characteristics." On the other hand, volunteered remarks revealed that "personality" played a strong part in defining leadership for those who supplied comments.

# Implications

This apparent paradox does not contradict the general understanding of how Americans feel about leadership. They react to the concept with desire and with fear. James MacGregor Burns has written that "One of the most universal cravings of our time is a hunger for compelling and creative leadership. We search eagerly for leadership yet seek to cage and tame it."[4] Future shock, a culture in transition, and massive societal problems engender yearnings for creative actions and reassurance that maybe there are, indeed, possible solutions, but the lessons of Hitler and Stalin are never far from the surface. We dearly cherish the democratic ethic which holds that a leader is a human among humans; that the leader is only the nucleus of a tendency or the human factor which binds a group together. These attitudes guide the way in which we regard leaders.

The library field, too, is in a transitional period, facing an uncertain future. Its community members, at least those responding to this survey, also exhibit contradictory emotions about leadership. Herb White, who has been mentioned once or twice this afternoon, commented recently that "The contradiction is perhaps best expressed in the realization that we believe in leaders and in leadership, but that on a personal basis few of us want to be led."[5] Phrased differently, people want to choose their leaders rationally, based on the content of their speeches and writings, not on the emotional quality of their presentation. On the other hand, delivery is an equal partner in communicating the message. The reasons librarians provided for nominating leaders illustrates the contradiction. When asked to choose from a list of pre-selected traits, reasons for naming people as leaders, their answers clearly indicated that what they most seek in a leader is the "Contribution of ideas." When given the option to elaborate upon their reasons, however, most of the volunteered comments had a substantial component which relates to "Personal characteristics."

Briefly, perceived leaders identified by respondents to this survey were chosen for their "ideas" and "visions." They have "Institutional positions" from which to transmit those ideas. They approach their tasks actively, courageously, and competently. And they eloquently advance their ideas both orally and in print.

# Notes

1. Kaufman and Jones in Dye, Thomas. *Who's Running America? Institutional Leadership in the United States.* Englewood Cliffs, N.J.: Prentice-Hall, 1976.
2. Rogers, Everett. *Diffusion of Innovations.* Glencoe, Ill.: Free Press, 1983, p. 34.
3. Stogdill, Ralph. *Stogdill's Handbook of Leadership.* Revised and expanded by Bernard Bass. New York: Free Press, 1981.
4. Burns, James MacGregor. 1978. *Leadership.* New York: Harper and Row, 1978, p. 1.
5. White, Herbert S. "Oh, Where Have All the Leaders Gone?" *Library Journal* 112 (16) Oct. 1, 1987, p. 68.

# Nurturing Leadership:
# A Personal View

*Robert Wedgeworth*

When Jana Varlejs called to ask me to be on the program this after-noon, it was my sense of responsibility and appreciation for what I gained from my years at Rutgers more than anything else that prompted me to accept because I'm still wondering what I think I know about the topic of this afternoon's symposium. I don't say that out of modesty. I do recognize that I have been fortunate enough in my career to have had the opportunity to serve in some leadership positions. But people in leadership positions don't spend a lot of time analyzing what leadership is. There are too many things on their plates that have to be devoured each day.

As I prepared for this talk, I kept asking myself, "Why is there such a concern for leadership—a concern that keeps popping up, over and over?" I think it's partly due to the "White Papers." Herb White has enormous influence. If I haven't read his column, I'm sure to have several people drop it on my desk as soon as *Library Journal* comes through the mail. I certainly would have to attribute some of the concern with leadership to Herb's treatment of the subject.

I would also relate the concern to something I learned at a dinner meeting I attended earlier this spring where the speaker was Gail Sheehy. As you know, Sheehy has been following around some of the candidates who would like to run for the presidency. She characterized the search for national leaders as a campaign in which there are so few ideas that we have to rely on factors like character. The same phenomenon, in a sense, has affected many different fields in this current period.

# The Changing Library Scene

As one of the speakers said earlier, there is a need for new direction in the field of library and information services. It is very common to talk about the uncertain days ahead and how difficult times are, and to question whether we are going to survive. I've never thought in terms like that — not about the library field or about anything else. There are matters over which we have little control.

What I have been working on lately, and getting excited by is a topic I have called "The Genius of North American Librarianship." I think there is a great deal to support the concept that I have been developing, although I'm beginning to feel a little bit self-conscious about choosing to look for genius in a field that has been a perennial academic underdog. Fortunately, I don't have to justify selecting librarianship because I think I have been providing that justification all of my life.

The two and a half decades that we have experienced prior to today have been among the most dramatic in the history of our field. I would say that probably the only more dramatic change in librarianship occurred during the period between 1886 and 1923 during the Carnegie philanthropy when Carnegie and the foundation he endowed gave so much money to American, British and Canadian communities that he virtually established the library field. I don't think we have seen a comparable period until the last 25 years when we have experienced great changes driven by technological innovations.

Along with the changes that have occurred in libraries, we have had dramatic sociological changes in our country as well as economic ones. I can recall, as an acquisitions librarian in the late 1960s, having to deal with currency fluctuations for the first time. There was great confusion. No one had ever had to deal with variable currency because the dollar had been strong and stable during the postwar years. Considered against a longer span of history, however, we're beginning now to live what I consider to be a normal economic life where currency fluctuations are common.

These general comments are intended to demonstrate that we have come through a period of enormous change. I think we're in the process of catching our breath. One of the legacies — deficiencies — of that period of change is that, although we made enormous investment in libraries and information services in the field, we made no comparable investment in our professional schools — the places where we expect to nurture leadership and the places we look to for research on these very same institutions and their services. This also is a contributing factor to the concern about future leadership. When we need the schools most, we perceive that they are not as strong as they ought to be to respond to the demands.

## Leader Qualities

You've heard from two speakers about past research into leadership. Although the studies they describe draw many distinct conclusions, little understanding of the nature of leadership and its essential components has been revealed. I've been most impressed by Warren Bennis' 1985 study in which he concentrates on the importance of vision and the importance of communication as two of the major strategic factors involved in leadership.

Most of the leadership studies that I have seen give a fairly low rating to "knowledge." I question that finding. I believe, rather, that what is being said is not that knowledge isn't important, but that we assume a certain level of knowledge and understanding to be associated with a leadership position. Therefore, a heavy emphasis on knowledge as a component of leadership seems unnecessary. Knowledge is one of the working tools you must have in order to exert leadership.

My experience leads me to focus on certain attributes, or leadership qualities, that I think can be discerned when we look for students, or when, in my various administrative capacities, we look for employees. It has also caused me to examine my own development.

I would say that power is a much underrated factor of leadership. In the library field we tend to think of power in an authoritative sense. Power means the authority to make things happen. That does not characterize the way things occur in our field. You may not have the authority to direct someone to do something, but you can influence individuals and groups to achieve specific ends.

This is really at the heart of my concept of the genius of North American librarianship. I contend that North American librarians have created larger, more elaborate, collaborative organizations than we have known ever before in this society, with governance mechanisms that would defy most management theorists. But they work. And that is indeed the genius in my opinion: that we have combined institutional initiative with large-scale professional collaboration.

This use of influence as a way of manifesting power is really the driving force behind those collaborative organizations. Take, for instance, the influence of an OCLC, or a Washington Library Network or the Network Advisory Committee of the Library of Congress. These organizations never had the authority to tell anyone to do anything. Yet, they were able to compel and persuade many institutions and many individuals to follow a given model in order to achieve an end that the community as a whole felt to be desirable. I think this is at the heart of the genius of North American librarianship.

I have to come back to some very fundamental leadership qualities that I think are often overlooked. Confidence is one such trait. An essential component of leadership is the ability to express ideas, possibilities, vision, with confidence. If you behave tentatively or indicate that you're not really sure that an ideal will work, people will not be persuaded.

I can recall, for example, when I was in elementary school — in the sixth grade. I was asked to run for mayor of the elementary school, a position traditionally held by a seventh grader. Our grade didn't like the seventh grade class and we decided to put up our own candidate. I was chosen as the sacrificial candidate. Everyone was sure that the sixth grader would lose. However, I had a little ace in the hole. I prevailed on my neighbor to help me fashion a full-fledged political campaign.

My opponent had decided that he was going to run on a platform to bring Coke into the elementary school cafeteria. Now I knew that those students were not fools. They were aware that the school would never allow them to bring a Coke machine into the cafeteria. Therefore, I ran, and won, on a platform which promoted the values of milk. The students had an opportunity, then, to vote for something that, while not preferable in their eyes, was realistic and not a losing proposition they knew could never be implemented. Now remember, I was confident that the school wouldn't permit Coke machines and I was confident that the students understood that the school would never permit Coke machines in that building. That's the kind of confidence I refer to now.

I will cite one other personal reference here. I was interviewed in January of 1972 by a group of people, only two of whom I knew, for a job which had been described as virtually impossible. The job was to run a large educational association that had, seemingly, enormous political troubles, and, according to *Library Journal,* might not survive. As I talked more and more to this group, I began to understand that they didn't really know exactly what was necessary to run the organization. That gave me the confidence to put forth my own tentative ideas about the nature of this organization and how support for its continuation might be mobilized.

# Translating Vision to Reality

Almost anyone in the leadership position gets those kinds of opportunities over and over and over again. Seizing upon them, I think, distinguishes those who are able to put forth a vision and turn it into reality and those who are managed by the events and circumstances that affect them. I believe that leadership lies very much in the ability to translate a vision into reality.

In 1977, Eric Moon and I went to England to help the Library Association celebrate its centennial. There we had a discussion about whether the chief executive officer of the national association should come from the profession or whether it should be a national leader drawn from the ranks of the cultural/academic community. Those are the two models that are followed by the respective associations. The British Library Association tends to choose a well-known scholar, public servant, or author to lead its organization as president. The American Library Association has traditionally drawn from the library profession for both its presidents and its chief executive officer. In the discussion, Eric and I tried to point out that knowledge of the culture and history and development of the field are essential to taking advantage of opportunities as they present themselves. If a leader has to say "Wait a minute, I have to consult with my colleagues," the opportunities may be lost. It may seem like a minor point, but I think it an extremely significant one with respect to national leadership of major organizations.

We don't talk enough about ambition. I don't mean ambition to be the "head" of something. I mean about what you will frequently find among persons in leadership positions—the ambition to make a difference, to make a significant contribution, to make things happen. That kind of ambition has to be present and represents one of the key driving forces of leadership. Ambition often is viewed negatively, as if there is something wrong with the person who wants to perform well.

Ambition is one of the key qualities that I look for in students with whom I want to work closely. I seek people who take pride in their work, who will do a job and feel confident that they've done it well. I want people who are not necessarily looking for public recognition but for whom the important fact is knowing that they've done something well.

Recently I had the opportunity to read Mary Gaver's autobiography, *The Braided Cord* (Scarecrow, 1988). Gaver is a retired professor from the Rutgers Graduate School of Library Service. Like others who will read the book, I flipped quickly to the key chapters to see what Mary had to say about this or that person or this or that institution. Mary did not always get along with all of her colleagues here at Rutgers. That was no secret!

The pages of Mary's autobiography are filled with the kind of ambition to serve and to lead and to make things happen that I have been describing. You can sense it from the time she was a young woman. This is the quality that you find frequently among leaders.

Communication is a much used concept in relation to leadership. I want to distinguish, however, between being articulate — being able to address a crowd — and communicating with a purpose in mind. What I am speaking about is planned communication to targeted audiences. Whenever you are in a position to say something to an individual or a group, you want to know what it is you wish to get across, or, alternately, what you want the other person to reveal to you. Sometimes you hear it characterized as "He or she doesn't waste your time when you're in a meeting." They communicate with a purpose, and that communication — though it may have been planned only five minutes before they walked into the meeting — that communication is to a targeted audience, and is what makes the communication effective.

## Nurturing Leadership

How do you nurture leadership from an educational perspective? This is a question I've been asked frequently. Let me just share a few general guidelines that I think are important. As I said, knowledge is underrated. I think it is fundamental. We want students who come to Columbia to have demonstrated that they are generally educated persons.

We consider a variety of other factors to try to determine whether this student really knows something he can build upon. We look for skills, while recognizing that an obligation of our program is to build skills. The kinds of skills we will be developing in the future will be somewhat different than the skills that were imparted when I was a student in Library School or when I was teaching in Library School. This is not to denigrate the quality of education that was offered by past graduate programs. It simply means that times have changed. The job today demands more methodological skills, more analytical skills, better knowledge of statistics in order to address complex problems and arrive at feasible solutions.

We will still be looking, however, for students who are ambitious to do well in the profession. We will still be looking for students who are confident, even cocky. We want that kind of student because that student is used to performing and feeling good about performing well. We want to help these students select positions which will provide important mentoring experiences. Someone asked me once how I mentor people. I don't think that I have been very much of a mentor in my life, but I do know that I sought mentoring situations in my career. I never took a job where I didn't think I'd have something to learn from someone or from the situation. I say the same thing to students. Don't work in a job where you don't feel that someone there can really teach you something.

There are two special factors that I learned from my family. One I call WDCW, which translated means "Willing to Defy Conventional Wisdom." Standard rules have become standard rules because they make good sense. Time and circumstances, however, can change, as can options. You have to be willing to take other options when you feel confident that they are appropriate.

The second is labeled URCS, which means an "Uncommon Reverence for Common Sense." You can get involved in extremely complex situations where you stay up nights trying to figure out what is the proper solution. Sometimes it helps to step back from a potential solution and say "It just doesn't make sense." If it doesn't make sense, then most of the time it's probably not going to work. That's what I call having an uncommon reverence for common sense. That kind of governor is important.

John Hersey, the author, once told me that when he was doing his series of interviews with the presidents, Harry Truman had one characteristic that really stood out. He seemed to have a little governor that told him very sharply and clearly when something was not right to do. Hersey described how he was invited to a meeting one evening with President Truman and some government officials talking about a member of the Senate, McCarthy, and about what they could do about him exposing people and making allegations that were either untrue or only partly true. At one point, one member of the group volunteered that he had information tht he could reveal about McCarthy which would completely discredit the Senator. Hersey said that at that point Truman, who had sat quietly listening to the discussion, interrupted. He ruled out any effort to discredit the Senator in this way and the discussion moved on to another topic. That kind of common sense is important.

# Character

It brings to mind once again what I talked about earlier — that reporters are falling back on character because there are no ideas in the campaign. Character is important. You don't like to do business with people you don't trust. Trust isn't developed instantly. It's based on understanding a pattern of behavior which people have demonstrated over a period of time. The most complex negotiation I've ever been involved in, the one to build Huron Plaza in Chicago, was concluded with a handshake. We had a legal contract, but that was developed later. One of my staff members asked me: "How could you go into something that complex and just assume that it's going to happen before you have a contract?" I answered: "If you don't trust someone, the best contract in the world won't help you." The important thing is to arrive at an understanding where there is mutual benefit. That's the essence of a contract, with legal language added. The other person wants this as much as we want it, and that's what is going to make it happen. Character is extremely important in leadership. People want to follow those they trust; people of quality whose values they share.

Character is developed at home; it is developed at school; it is developed in a network of friendships. And the character you develop stays with you.

As Gail Sheehy said: "By the time that leaders get into positions of leadership their character is sown and the destiny they reap is our own."

# Women and Minorities as Leaders

*Emily R. Mobley*

As I was sitting here listening to the high level research being presented, I thought, "My God, this is going to be a hard act to follow." However, one of the traits of a leader, as Bob Wedgeworth pointed out, is self-confidence. I will confidently move into my topic from a practicing librarian's viewpoint.

## Leadership Concepts

I did some investigation of the concept of leadership, performed literature searches in various areas and looked at some of the writings in the field. It was a frustrating experience – due both to the paucity of information *and* to the volume of information. The problem seems inherent in leadership and in the difficulties in defining the term. Stogdill states it succinctly: "There are almost as many definitions of leadership as there are persons who have attempted to define the concept."[1] The basic difficulty in definition stems from whether one looks at leadership broadly, considering it an occurrence of some modification of behavior or performance by a group due to the interaction of one or more members of the group; or whether one restricts the definition to the personal traits associated with leadership. My previous work on leadership has always started from the premise that leadership is related to personal traits and most importantly that leadership and management should be separated in discussions of leadership. My concept has been summed up, again by Stogdill, in this statement: "Leaders must manage and managers must lead, but the two are not synonymous."[2] Herb White, with whom I rarely find myself in agreement, accurately – this time—described leadership in the article we are using as today's theme. He wrote: "Leadership skills are not the same as management skills."[3] Many, on the other hand, disagree with the trend toward separating management and leadership. The majority of literature describing leadership is based on what can be termed managerial leadership, and a great volume of literature it is! In fact, regardless of my premise or my definition of leadership, it was necessary for me to look at leadership from a managerial aspect if I hoped to say more than a few words today.

Another of the debates centering around leadership addresses the question of whether leadership is intrinsic or whether it can be learned. A relatively new book, *The Leadership Challenge,*[4] offers readers instruction in how to learn leadership behaviors. Peter Drucker, too, disagrees with the premise that leadership is intrinsic. In a *Wall Street Journal* article published in January of this year, he wrote: "there [are no] such things as leadership qualities or a leadership personality."[5]

When one looks at the literature which discusses leadership from a perspective of personality traits, one notices that women are missing from the discussion, and very little appears about minorities. Even the very comprehensive chapters on "Women and Leadership" and "Blacks and Leadership" in *Stogdill's Handbook of Leadership* reflect this fact. There seems to be some substance to the criticism that the current model of leadership is only relevant to white males.

## Women and Minorities in Leadership Positions

The issues surrounding women and minority leadership in the library field are essentially a microcosm of issues in the society in general. The problem for women is exacerbated by the fact that although the percentage of women in the profession stands at about 80, the ratio of female to male library leaders and top administrators is not 8 to 10.

While no recent comprehensive statistical studies have produced data on the racial composition of librarians, a new study on minority library school graduates[6] between 1979 and 1984 shows a decrease from 9.6 percent in 1979 to 6 percent in 1984. In 1982 and 1983, the percentage actually dipped below 6 percent. In 1984, the percentage of black library school graduates was 2.7, a substantial decrease from the 4.5 percent in 1979. However, the number of leaders, or at least the number of administrative positions held by minorities, more closely approximates their representation in the profession than do the numbers for women.

In looking at the current situation of women and minorities in leadership positions in general, one finds a dearth of women and minorities in management or administrative roles from which leadership opportunities emerge. Of course this results from past sexual and racial discrimination practices and will still require a number of years before the imbalance is rectified. Unfortunately, however, there is general consensus that the gains made in the 1960s and 1970s are not keeping pace today. In fact, retrenchment is evident. There is a reversal in the trend toward greater numbers of women and minorities in positions which lead to the boardrooms of corporate America. Women hold only 2 percent of the senior executive corporation posts in the United States.[7] Only three of the Fortune 1000 companies have a woman as chief executive.[8] Only one has a black.[9] And these are 1988 figures! Thus, in today's world, only 4 of the top 1000 — that is four-tenths of one percent — of the companies in the United States have a woman or black at the helm. As one writer stated: "the concept of women as corporate leaders is just that — a concept."[10] Obviously the same can be said of minorities.

Academe has done better, but by no means is there near equality between the sexes and races. A new survey by the American Council on Education of the chief executive officers in over 2,000 colleges and universities[11] found that 296, or 14 percent, of the institutions are headed by women. But of these 296, 40 percent head women's colleges. Seven percent of the presidents of institutions of higher education are members of minority groups. Five percent, or 100, are blacks, and half of the blacks head historically black colleges. When those who head women's or black institutions are not considered, the gender and racial imbalance is increased. Retrenchment in the numbers of women moving into chief executive officer positions in academe is also evident. Between 1975 and 1984, there was a 20 percent increase in the number of women presidents every three years. However, in the last triennial survey — 1984–1987 — the growth rate fell to 3.5 percent. Thus, higher education reflects the current national slowdown in the amount of ground women are gaining. Since 80 percent of current college presidents held previous positions as presidents of other institutions, vice-presidents, deans, or directors, if women are not moving into these positions, then it is unlikely that women will be moving into presidencies.

It is no mystery why the advancement of women and minorities into top positions is moving at a snail's pace and even falling back from that pace. We are still in an era of the "old-boy's network" and specifically the "old white boy's network." And believe me they are fighting to keep their network intact. We are still dealing with the prevalent attitude of only being comfortable with "like." Thus, only "like" have any opportunity of success. Few women and minorities make it to the top. There are not enough of them to help change stereotypes, to educate the old boys, and make them comfortable with women as anything but wives, daughters, secretaries, and lovers; and with blacks as anything but gardeners, maids and chauffeurs. Thus women and minorities continue to end up in support level managerial positions and not line management positions where decisions which have impact on the vital interests of the organization are made.

## The Library Field

Libraries as organizations are not institutions unto themselves. Academic, special, government and school libraries are parts of larger organizations. The public library is beholden to a city manager, a council, mayor, or to some other organization. Thus, the director of a library most often reports to whom else but one of the old boys because the top executive and managerial ranks are still dominated by them. And they, of course, prefer to deal with one of their own. The larger the parent organization, the more likely it is to be headed by a white male, whether it is a university, corporation, public school system, or government agency. It comes as no surprise, therefore, that in a profession which is 80 percent female, the directorships are still held by white males, particularly in large libraries. All statistics point to the fact that regardless of the type of organization, the greatest percentage of women managers, administrators, or directors head smaller departments, schools, or institutions than men, even within the same parent organization.

The statistics from the Association of Research Libraries[12] support the above statements. In fiscal year 1988, only 28 of 103, 27 percent of the directors of ARL libraries are female. In every other position, except heads of special collections and computer departments, there are more women than men. In traditional "support" departments such as cataloging and acquisitions, the ratio of female to male department heads is two to one. As dire as these current statistics are, only four years ago 18 of the 94, 19 percent, of ARL directors were female. The 1988 survey shows that only two directors are minority group members. One is male and the other female. There has been one increase since then—a male. Let us hope that the customary procedure of filling directorships from the ranks of associate and assistant directors continues in the future. Fifty-six percent of these positions are currently held by women, and five percent are occupied by minorities.

I can't resist adding a comment about salaries. The salaries of men average almost 13 percent higher than the salaries of women in ARL libraries for 1988. While the number of men in higher paying positions may, to some extent, account for this discrepancy, it should be noted that even those males with less than five years' experience also have consistently higher salaries than women, although the percentage of difference is not as great. In that case, it runs between three and five percent.

I do not have comparable statistics for special libraries, but some observations seem justified. There is a tendency for the largest special libraries to be headed by men. There is also a tendency for males to head those library or information centers which have been accorded responsibility for nontraditional library functions that are intimately related to the welfare of the organization. The position of corporate information officer, a new title which has arisen in recognition of the importance of information to the strategic management of a corporation, is almost always held by a male, and a male who is generally not a librarian by education. Corporate information officers are usually line management positions on an executive instead of a managerial level.

## *Leadership of the Professional Associations*

Barbara Ivy[13] approached the question of how important power is in the director hiring process by looking at the relative weights attached to various items which might appear on a resume. Of the five variables Ivy identified, the two most important are *power within the position* and *power within the profession.* Ivy evaluated power within the position in this context by looking at the importance placed on recommendations from within an applicant's current institution, the candidate's current position title, and institutional assignments outside the library. She evaluated power within the profession in terms of the importance accorded recommendations from influential librarians outside the candidate's current institution, elected offices held in professional organizations and publications in professional journals or books, and awards and honors and so forth from professional organizations. Ivy found a significant relationship between the size of the institution and the value placed on the power within the profession when hiring a new library director. Thus national reputation is power. Recommendations from leaders in the field which result from leadership of a professional organization become an important element in gaining entry to the ranks of directors of large academic libraries.

Due to the importance Ivy attached to professional participation in the hiring process, I explored the issue of women and minority leadership by looking at the history of office holding, and in particular the presidency of the two largest United States library associations—the American Library Association and the Special Library Association. Each organization has a membership reflecting the sexual distribution within the profession. The ALA has been served by 100 presidents from 1876 to the present. Only 27, 27 percent, have been women. Twelve women, or a little less than half of the group, were elected within the last 20 years. The SLA has had 67 presidents since 1909. Thirty-four, or 50 percent, were women. ALA, of course, has a longer history. If the time span used for both organizations is made comparable, 1909–1988, the figures now reflect that 35 percent of the ALA presidents since 1909 were women. (There were no female presidents during the period 1876 to 1909 despite the presence of women in library schools and within libraries.) Only two blacks have been elected president of the American Library Association in its 112-year history, while three blacks have served as SLA president in the 79 years of that organization.

The outcome of this exercise is surprising as there is a significant difference in the percentage of female leadership in SLA compared with the percentage of female leadership in ALA. As the greatest numbers of SLA members have always been corporate librarians, employed in male-dominated environments, the results seem even more surprising. One plausible explanation for this difference may be that male librarians in corporate situations have had numerous leadership opportunities in other professional organizations whose doors were closed to women, thus leaving the positions in the library association to women. Another explanation may be that those women who gravitated to the special library field exhibited leadership traits similar to those of males. Women, after all, were an anomaly in professional positions in corporations. It may have been natural for a great number of these women to assume leadership roles within a professional organization because they had developed the skills and the know-how to survive within their own corporation.

## Career Patterns

In both the corporate and academic sectors, the importance of mentoring as a method of increasing the representation of women and minorities in the highest ranks has been discussed by a number of authors. It must be stressed that mentoring is important for increasing the numbers of females and minorities in leadership positions in librarianship. Here is where leadership and management become one in the professional environment. Evidence of leadership in a profession may result in more opportunities to succeed to a higher managerial level. However, if one does not reach a relatively higher managerial level early in one's career, opportunities to be considered for leadership positions in the profession are relatively few. It is a double-edged sword which mentoring can help to blunt. The women and minorities who have achieved national reputations as leaders and the old-boys who've always been there must take an active role in the process in order to promote effective equality of opportunity for future leaders. I'm pleased to see, and to be a part of, the evidence that this is occurring, but such activity must increase.

On the other hand, women and minorities must actively seize opportunities which provide potential access to positions of leadership. A number of years ago when I was recruited for a job at General Motors corporation, I was turned off by the fact that (they were very honest with me) they would like a minority employee, and being a woman would certainly not hurt and, furthermore, I had impeccable qualifications. We played a cat and mouse game for nine months. Finally I asked myself, "What is the problem here? The problem is — I don't like the fact that I'm being singled out, because of affirmative action, as someone you wish to hire. On the other hand, what will that position do for my career? What will it do for my leadership potential?" So I took the job. My next move was to General Motors Institute. My colleagues thought my decision the "ultimate risk" since the corporation had just announced that it would divest itself of the Institute. But again I reflected upon what the job would do for me. The position was director of the Institute Library. I thought that even if the Institute were to fold sometime later, I would have gained another set of credentials which could serve as a springboard to a better job. I can say to you quite sincerely that had I not taken some of these risks, I would not be standing before you today, talking on this topic. I would not have achieved or been able to achieve a position of leadership. Leadership is always risk-taking.

Joanne spoke about the relationship between leaders and committee participation. Women too frequently serve, willingly, on committees. They function as team members. When it comes to taking charge, however, or holding elective office or even risking running for election, they are unwilling to accept the responsibility. Women need to consider carefully the importance of competing for those important positions.

Statistics have indicated that librarianship has not followed yet the retrenchment patterns in the number of women assuming leadership positions evident in other professions. The same is not true for minority representation. Library leaders must accept the challenge of "bucking" the trends of society in general and continue to push on.

# Notes

1. Stogdill, Ralph. *Stogdill's Handbook of Leadership.* Revised and expanded by Bernard Bass. New York: Free Press, 1981, p. 7.
2. *Ibid.*, p. 273.
3. White, Herbert S. "Oh, Where Have All the Leaders Gone?" *Library Journal* 112 (Oct. 1, 1987): 69.
4. Kouzes, James, and Barry Pozner. *The Leadership Challenge: How to Get Extraordinary Things Done in Organizations.* San Francisco: Jossey-Bass, 1987.
5. Drucker, Peter. "Leadership: More Doing Than Dash." *Wall Street Journal,* 6 January 1988.
6. Brown, Lorene B. "A Crisis in Leadership: The Decline in the Number of Minorities Entering the Profession Since 1979, Summary Statistics." Paper presented to the Black Caucus of the American Library Association, January 19, 1986.
7. "Women Make Slow Progress Up the Corporate Ladder." *Economist* 302 (March 14, 1987): 61.
8. *Ibid.*
9. Leinster, Colin. "Black Executives: How They're Doing" *Fortune* 117 (January 18, 1988): 109.
10. Evans, Jane. "Will Women Lead?" *Management World* 12 (December 1983): 1.
11. "The College President." *Chronicle of Higher Education* 34 (March 30, 1988): A14–15, 22.
12. ARL *Annual Salary Survey, 1987.* Washington, D.C. Association of Research Libraries, 1988.
13. Ivy, Barbara A. "Identity, Power and Hiring in a Feminized Profession." *Library Trends* 28 (Fall 1985): 291–308.

# Where Is the Next Generation of Leaders?

## Panel and Audience Discussion

**Euster:** I'd like to start the discussion with a question: Where is the next generation of leaders coming from? I'm willing to risk a position statement and then I'll stand back.

I really think we have to rethink our definition of leadership. Bob Wedgeworth's comments on the collaborative nature of librarianship in North America are particularly germane here. We need to develop leadership among people for future authority positions, but we also, and more importantly, need to recognize that leaders, people of power, are found in many positions and in many roles in the library world, and pay attention to what I think is nearly universal leadership development. This is a responsibility, not just of the library schools, but of all of us in the profession.

**Wedgeworth:** The leadership that we're looking for is leadership of a special kind, caused partially from uncertainty in the field. Leaders are going to come from the same place as they've always come from. I found the director of the Salt Lake City Public Library in a tiny town in Ohio where he had persuaded the community to invest in building a new library. They were so proud of it, just bursting, and, ten years later, he is the director of one of the finest public library systems in the nation. Leaders will emerge from among the people who are solving some of the technical problems that will enable us to interconnect the networks. Who's going to be the next Henriette Avram? I think she's already there. But we don't recognize her because we are looking for people with messages and answers.

The people who have a track record of performance are out there. We just have to open our eyes and look for them. They're not out there giving visionary scenarios about the future of the field. That's what you do when you are in the position, and the ability to do it comes from the background and training that you acquired in doing other kinds of things.

Leaders are there. They've got the track record, and they are going to be identified as candidates for important library positions. And then when they get into those positions, suddenly the fact that they have vision will become clear.

Identifying leadership potential is like identifying outstanding students. We want students with a track record; we want students who have confidence; we look for students who want to make a difference in terms of their careers and in terms of their lives. Those people are out there, and they come from the same backgrounds that earlier generations of leaders have come from. They have come from the technical areas of the field; they have come from the user services areas; and more and more they have come from general managerial areas.

**Gertzog:** I approach the matter from a slightly different perspective. I think the leaders will come, in the way that Bob says, from a variety of sources because we need different kinds of leaders. We need leaders who are innovators, and therefore we will produce some of those. We need leaders who will lead by virtue of the situation. I think that leaders must be able to be boundary spanners, to look at the field as a whole or the particular institution in its entirety and determine how the parts fit together, rather than looking at them separately. I think we will find that those are the people who provide the most leadership. Often they are not associated with particular libraries, but with associations, or journals, or consortia—a variety of places. New kinds of training grounds for leaders exist in the library field.

**Leslie Burger,** New Jersey State Library: A major part of my responsibility with the State Library is to create opportunities for library leadership for New Jersey librarians. We are embarking on a program to provide some specific training in the kind of leadership skills all of you have alluded to today. We're planning a 30-person, six-day institute which will include structured types of experiences designed to expose participants to leadership skills. Specifically, they will receive communication training, and instruction in how to use power and influence in specific situations. Our intention is to continue this on an annual basis in order to nurture leaders within a structure where we can be both teaching skills as well as creating the networks that people need to support leadership within the profession.

**Betty Turock,** Rutgers: In your findings, Alice, it seems to me that you indicated that the "contribution of ideas" was important to librarians' perceptions of leadership, but that the educator role was not, or at least not as important. From that I might say that the perception of the educator in the "contribution of ideas" may be minimal, or to use Bob's argument, that the conventional wisdom would say that the real problem is that educators have difficulty in diffusion of knowledge to the field. It is my feeling that the university educator in library education is not making the kind of contribution that he or she might to ideas in the profession. If that is the case in an environment which has as its major mission the contribution of ideas, I'd like to ask the panel what they think is occurring that stifles that contribution. I hope your comments might include more than the fact that the library educators are not retooled.

**Gertzog:** Before I am misquoted, I hope I did not say that educators are not seen as contributing ideas, but rather that it seemed to me that people who responded to the survey considered leaders to be those who are policy rather than academically oriented. However, let me follow that with some thoughts. I do not disagree with you. I think we have seen, and my research seems to support it, a bifurcation of the field—a split between the academic and the practitioner. Even in some of the responses I received to my survey, there was an underlying hostility—a hostility toward answering questionnaires, a hostility toward "people in their ivory towers." "Why don't you do something practical?" some asked. I really did think that the identification of leaders, and some understanding of emergent leadership, was practical. But obviously some of my respondents did not.

The split does exist and is extremely real. It stems, partially at least, from the way in which we educate MLS students. We do not educate them to ideas at a sufficiently high level. Therefore the people who become leaders are boundary spanners, the ones who translate what has happened in the academy to the profession because the information does not travel directly from the educator/researchers themselves to the practitioners.

**Mobley:** My response to that question is only in terms of the special library. The question is beyond merely retooling. Retooling is needed so that educators understand the environment in which we are practicing. The other problem is the way that educators look at research. I would like to see educators look at research on more than one level and not only the empirical or scholarly level. Some of the research that is needed is at the point of practice. We can't always wait for two or three years until a rigorous study is done. Therefore we need to think of research at, perhaps, three different levels. But we need to be able to know the difference between which type needs to be undertaken.

**Wedgeworth**: I'd like to speak up for educators. I can do that because I don't consider myself one. I just ask you, how much of a contribution you think junior faculty members who should be our most productive idea producers can make when they've got to teach five courses a year, with perhaps four preparations for those five courses. They have to teach in summer school in order to make ends meet because they've got families to support. I think you need to look at the fact that the institutions educating our graduates have average budgets of about $600,000. And if you compare these departments to other academic departments, they're just tiny, tiny units within most major universities.

During the period when librarians were developing all these major systems that we're so proud of at the local, state and regional levels, nobody really thought about carving out 1 percent or 2 percent of that money and putting it into developing some research capacity. One of the most productive periods of library education was when Office of Education Fellowships were available that produced some of the top researchers that we have in the field today. Those researchers are now mature, and the question remains: Where will the next generation of young researchers as educators come from? If we want that kind of productivity from our library schools, we've got to be willing to make an investment. We've got to have people in the field stand up and say this investment needs to be made. To ask educators why they aren't contributing more is an inappropriate question. If the kind of flexibility within budgets was available to library schools that exists within libraries — and I know you don't have much — I think we would see a lot more production. But it just isn't there.

**Anne Mintz,** Forbes Magazine Library: I don't know that you can look for leadership from your student body and define who your leaders are going to be. Grades don't tell the story. I've been considered a leader in special libraries, for example, but I don't think I stood out at Rutgers when I was a student. I don't think you can look at the records of a graduate student who may be under financial pressure, taking courses, perhaps working full time. I, as an employer, do not use records as a barometer when I am interviewing master's degree students as candidates for future employment. I have interviewed people for ten years now to work with me. What I tend to look for are personality characteristics. Can this person stand up and tell my boss that what he wants does not exist? Does this candidate understand that the person who is your client is the one you have to be able to address as a colleague.

I look for people who are no more afraid during the interview than I am on the other side of the desk. I look for people who have that certain kind of self-confidence. Some people simply do not test well.

**Euster:** An anecdote! One of the evaluations of me at the time when I graduated from library school at the University of Washington said: "Miss Euster is a competent, quiet and unassuming young woman who will do well in public service!"

**Danilo Figueredo,** Executive Director, New Jersey Libraries: I have two questions. One concerns the issue of recruitment, at all levels of the library world, including the most basic, attracting students to library school. I have a friend who recruits for AT&T. When her recruiting table is next to someone recruiting for libraries, that person does not do as well as my friend. Entry level salaries at AT&T are much higher than entry level salaries in libraries, despite the fact that libraries require a master's degree and the jobs for which my friend recruits require only a BA degree.

I have experienced this, also, when I worked with organizations trying to recruit Hispanic students into higher education. Once again these corporations are a tough act to follow. I wonder if this is something you have encountered, and if it represents a national trend. Is this something library schools in the country are looking into?

The other question is based on a very personal observation, and not a scientific study. It seems to me that once individuals, including minority individuals, reach a certain level, they begin to dress alike, behave in a certain similar manner and know the same people. I remember hearing it said that as you advance and succeed in our society, those things that make you different — class or ethnic background — tend to disappear. I have noticed in certain people that if that ethnic background has not disappeared altogether, they seem to exhibit two personalities, one ethnic and one not. Once they get to ALA or a particular association meeting, the ethnic personality disappears. Have you found this? Is this something good or bad? Does it make a difference?

**Mobley:** I can only say that your perceptions — about both questions — are true. I am speaking from a personal perspective. Let me address the last question first. I call it schizophrenia. In fact I actually warn young blacks in colleges that part of being successful means having to be very good at living with schizophrenia. There was a very poignant article in *Essence* magazine about five or six years ago written by a black woman just before she committed suicide in which she describes this very problem, the schizophrenia that occurs from being a minority in a majority society.

On your first point, I'm often contacted by people, who have money, for help in identifying blacks who may be interested in going to school. In my conversations with potential students, I find there is not much of an interest in going into the library field, or as much as one would like. Part of the reason is that there are so many other fields open. At one time, librarianship was one of the fields not closed to minorities. But everything else has opened up. I can say to you honestly that I am not sure whether or not I would be standing here in front of you today if, when I was 18 years old, the opportunities were the way they are now.

**Wedgeworth**: I think the first thing we have to recognize is that both of these are very natural tendencies. Virtually every ethnic group that has been documented in this country has gone through the same kind of transformation. The difference is that we today somehow feel that those persons we identify as minorities shouldn't live more than one life. Well, I don't talk to you the way that I talk to my family when I go to Kansas City. I certainly don't talk to you the way I talk with my friends from childhood. There are things that we shared as children, as a family, that are very distinct. I think the important thing is for people to have a good sense of who they are.

You have to be willing to laugh at yourself. My favorite all-time book is Ralph Ellison's *Invisible Man*. It's a tragic book, but there is humor in Ellison's description of how people look at you. To them you are somehow different. They don't believe you ever had a mother, a father, brothers, sisters, or high school friends. They don't believe you are like the people they go to work with every day.

Most of us live multiple lives. Why should this be considered a negative concept? I think it enriches us. It is a part of our character. You are absolutely right. Your comment is on target. But I don't view it as a negative. We wouldn't want a person who undertakes a national office, or moves into a major position, to act as if he or she were "on the block." There's nothing wrong with "on the block." Holding a position of power and influence, however, places you in a structured situation which requires different behavior in order to perform the job successfully. The structure is different and therefore you must act differently.

My friends with whom I shared my childhood knew when they came to my office in Chicago to meet me that they would be treated differently there than they would be in my home. That's normal.

The other question deals with a situation which you have accurately described. In the early days when the second generation immigrant families went to college, what did they study? They chose those professions that would give them security and higher prestige than the kinds of occupations with which their parents had been associated. They chose to become accountants; they chose to become doctors; they chose to become attorneys. I think it's happening right now. Remember, we in the library profession are not drawing from an undergraduate population. We are trying to attract college graduates. These minority students have already achieved a substantial amount considering many of their family and ethnic backgrounds. Consequently they are sought after from many professional sectors and they have available to them a wide variety of career choices.

The question is not why more of them may want to go to AT&T than want to have careers as librarians, but can we be sure that we get our share of those students who may want to enter a career of public service, who may want a career which is intellectually stimulating, with possibilities for advancing faster than the network that Emily Mobley was describing? There are attributes of our profession that can and should be positively sold, instead of bemoaning our lack of ability to attract students. Students want different things from their lives and careers. The question is can we find the match between what our career choice offers and what their background and interests may motivate them towards?

**Marc Eisen**, Assistant Director, East Orange Public Library: I'm concerned about some of the personality questions that have been raised. I'm trying to tie them together. Alice's research showed that comments about leaders tended to relate to personality, and Bob mentioned leaders' willingness to defy conventional wisdom.

Thirty years ago, my New York City high school social studies Regent's Exam required an essay on the proposition that progress is only created by iconoclasts who defy the conventional wisdom. Anybody who accepts it makes no progress in the world. When I was in library school, I was required to read an article in *Atlantic Monthly* entitled "Don't Give Us Your Tired, Your Poor." This week, the *New York Times* reported that some personality traits, most notably shyness, show up as early as infancy and cannot be changed at all.

In trying to tie all these together, I wonder whether there is a type of personality which chooses a library career in the first place, and that may, in fact, change some of the ways leaders rise to the top. Perhaps it explains to some extent the reasons for some of the racial and sexual differences compared to the population at large. There have been programs on Myers-Briggs personality types, I think. I don't know how library personalities relate to others or compare to other fields. I wonder if anybody has any comments on the type of personality in the library field and the impact on leadership.

**Euster**: There have been at least two studies I'm aware of that use standardized instruments to look at personality types. Based on their findings, we know that librarians as a whole are introverts, like to do their work, prefer things to be mechanical. Public service librarians tend to be slightly less so than technical service librarians, but on the whole we're all on the introverted side of the scale.

I took the Myers-Briggs recently and it revealed me to be an extrovert. That's not my self-concept! I had about a week of wandering around, muttering to myself, until I finally concluded — so I could go back to sleeping — that in fact I am to a large extent an introverted person who has learned to behave in an extroverted manner for certain purposes. In some way that supports Bob's contention that you are indeed different persons in different situations.

**Gertzog**: While we may be a profession of introverts, it is interesting to note that one of the earliest studies of occupational attitudes towards politics done in the late '30s or early '40s found that librarians, of all professional groups, were the most radical!!

# Thinking About Leadership

*Alice Gertzog*

Consideration of "leadership" over the centuries has centered on certain knotty problems which have been the subject of continuing debate. All students of "leadership" must confront and wrestle with these quesitons before embarking on any new investigation of the subject. But we should be aware of the dangers inherent in studying the topic. Aaron Wildavsky has warned that in the "disappearing act called leadership all paths . . . end up by swallowing their subject."[1]

Leadership is a universal human phenomenon.[2] All social structures have leaders.[3] Leadership involves a relationship between leader and group.[4] Beyond these three generalizations, which have been demonstrated through research, little that is definitive can be said about leadership. Most concepts of leadership do, however, generally assume an influence process whereby influence is exerted by the leader over followers.[5]

## The Problem of Definition

Although the word "leader" is found in the English language around the year 1300, the term "leadership" does not appear until about 1800. Definitionally the word leadership is ambiguous, perceptual and contextual. In addition, it is subject to changes over time. Some even question whether it is a useful concept. Stogdill maintained that there are as many definitions of leadership as there are people attempting to define it.[6] James McGregor Burns discovered 130 definitions while preparing his monumental study.[7] The absence of a precise, generally accepted definition of leadership compounds the difficulty of operationalizing it for purposes of conducting research. Gibb contended that the concept of leadership, like that of general intelligence, has largely lost its value for the social sciences . . . so diverse are [these] ways [of leading] that any one concept attempting to encompass them all, as leadership does, loses the specificity and precision necessary to scientific thinking.[8]

Barbara Kellerman describes the problem of definition in this way:

1) What is leadership? Getting people to follow. How many people? All the people all the time? By what means and to what ends? Is force a legitimate leadership tool?
2) Where is leadership exercised? In politics. But of course not all leadership takes place in the public sector, nor is the state the only unit with a leader at the head. Corporate (economic) leadership then? Religious leadership? Interpersonal leadership?
3) Who is the leader? The leader is the one who holds the highest office. Or is the leader the one with the most personal power of influence? Is the leader at the forefront? Or does the true leader in fact take cues from the led?
4) And who are the led? The led are most of us, at least some of the time. When? Under what circumstances?[9]

The *International Encyclopedia of the Social Sciences* treats leadership under three headings: psychology, sociology and political science. James MacGregor Burns describes how these and other disciplines approach the study of leadership:

**Historians** and biographers typically focus on the unique person with more or less idiosyncratic qualities and traits confronting particular sets of problems and situations over time.
**Psychologists** scrutinize genetic factors, early inter-family relationships, widening arcs of personal interaction, changing constellations of attitudes and motivations.
**Sociologists** view the developing personality as it moves through a series of social contexts — family, school, neighborhood, workplace — and undergoes powerful socializing forces in the process.
**Political Scientists** emphasize the social and political institutions impinging on developing leaders, changes in political leaders as they learn from experience, the eventual impact of leadership on policy and history.[10]

The important research into leadership being carried on by students of organizational behavior and organizational development should be mentioned as well. They tend to focus primarily on the relationship between task, leader and group member. In addition, historiometric research, which investigates the similarities in background and behavior of leaders, is beginning to develop some important insights into the nature of leaders.[11]

Other definitional problems emerge when attempts are made to distinguish between terms related to leadership such as power, persuasion, authority, influence, expertise, charisma and control.

## The Situation and Trait Controversy

An important debate in the study of leadership has centered on the "great man" versus "circumstance" controversy, elsewhere called the "trait (personality)" or "situation" argument. Sometimes the two sides are termed "role-determining" and "role-determined" or "event-making" and "eventful." No matter their labels, they all meet in the historic and often asked question: "Do the times make the leader or the leader the times?" Or, as Diana Crane has posed the quandary: Are scientific discoveries "the massive achievements of certain giant figures" or the logical outcome of a particular stage in the development of a field.[12]

The Great Man theory, or trait approach, which dates back to the ancient Greeks and Romans, was articulated as a concept in 1841 by Thomas Carlyle in *Heroes and Hero-Worship and the Heroic in History*.[13] This theory holds that there are certain individuals whose innate superiority marks them as natural leaders, and sets them apart from their followers. For instance, Moses, Mohammed, Jesus and Calvin are seen as "solitary, dramatic figures who mobilized and inspired masses to new goals and methods of religious salvation."[14] Carlyle actually argued that the history of the world is but the biography of great men, an assertion which was echoed by Ralph Waldo Emerson in his statement that "There is properly no history, only biography."[15]

Traits associated with leadership include physical ones such as energy, appearance and height; intelligence and ability traits; personality traits such as adaptability, aggressiveness, enthusiasm and self-confidence; task-related characteristics, such as achievement, drive, persistence and initiative; and nine social characteristics, among which are cooperativeness, interpersonal skills and administrative ability.[16]

Hitler and Mussolini are offered as extreme examples of the circumstance approach. Adherents to this school contend that leadership flourishes only in problem situations and "great leaders" are produced by time, place and circumstance. The situationist approach denies or minimizes the influence of individual difference.

Among the situational factors found to be related to leadership are 1) age and previous experience of the leader; 2) community in which the organization operates; 3) the particular work requirements of the group; 4) the psychological climate of the group being led; 5) the kind of job the leader holds; 6) the size of the group led; 7) the degree to which group member cooperation is required; 8) the cultural expectations of subordinates; 9) group members' personalities; and 10) time required and allowed for decision-making.[17]

Few would maintain that "situation" itself produces leadership. Apposite circumstances may be necessary, but they hardly seem sufficient. Most theorists now consider the person and situation within the context of the interactive effect of both. It is recognized that leaders may not emerge if the conditions or circumstances are unfavorable. In other words, many students of leadership consider that the characteristics required of leaders vary with their personalities, with task requirements, with the nature of the follower community, and with the organizational and physical environment.

The contingency school, an outgrowth of the combined situationist-trait theories, holds that

> leadership performance depends as much on the organization as it depends on the leader's own attributes. Except perhaps for the unusual case, it is simply not meaningful to speak of an effective leader or an ineffective one; we can only speak of a leader who tends to be effective in one situation and ineffective in another.[18]

## Learned or Inherent Leadership

Even those who subscribe to the "great man" theory can be divided into two schools. One holds that leaders are born. The other contends that they are the products of background and experience. In brief, it is the old nature-nurture argument.

The view that leaders are born, not trained, lost currency with the ascendancy of the behaviorist school of psychology. Behaviorists view only physical characteristics and perhaps a tendency toward good health as innate.

Those who adopt the latter position, the people who contend that socialization plays a major role in leadership, consider almost every one to have leadership potential, and, further, that the major competencies of leadership can be learned. Based on interviews with 90 leaders,

Warren Bennis concluded that he was "convinced that people can learn or teach themselves the skills of leadership."[19] Other students of leadership concur, and call leadership not a gift but a learned talent. These theorists conclude, therefore, that effective systems for training leaders can be devised.

Those who embrace the opposite position, that leadership is inborn, contend that leadership training, in reality, teaches nothing more than the skills of good management.

## Managers and Leaders

There has been a tendency to equate management and leadership. But many assume that one can be a leader and not a manager, just as one may be a manager without exercising leadership.

As far back as 1935, Pigors distinguished between "headship" and "leadership" citing as the prime difference between the two the *source* of the power to influence.[20] In formal organizations with appointed heads, the authority is vested from outside the group. The "head" has the authority of the larger organization. For "leaders," the authority is willingly accorded by group members. Headship and leadership are not necessarily mutually exclusive. Nor, however, are they mutually coincident as much of the current leadership and management literature seems to suggest.

Originally, authority for leadership was seen as coming from God, or subsequently from the innate nature of man. Rulers were legitimate. Authority arose from tradition, religious sanctions, rights of succession and procedures, not by the will of the people. Power was vested in the status as well as the person. This authoritarian model held that leaders have exclusive rights to command; subordinates or subjects must obey. After the 18th and 19th century democratic revolutions, power resided in the office, not the office holder. Followers became important, as did the awareness of group needs and rule by consent of the governed.

An important typology of leadership was constructed by Max Weber who isolated three kinds of legitimate authority:

> 1. **Traditional authority** is manifested by leaders who are empowered to rule based on their birth or class. Patriarchs and monarchs fall under this heading.
> 2. **Legal (or bureaucratic) authority** is applied to those who hold positions because of demonstrated technical competence.

3.  **Charismatic authority** describes those thought to be endowed with extraordinary, sometimes magical powers. Prophets, war heroes and demagogues fall under this rubric.[21]

## Charismatic Leadership

There is increasing contemporary interest surrounding the notion of charismatic leaders, those who have qualities often perceived as superhuman . . . or at least totally exceptional, which set them apart from all others.[22] Charismatic leaders' personal abilities render them able to engender a profound effect on followers.

Charismatic leaders have been found to have high self-confidence, to have a strong conviction in their own beliefs and ideals and a strong need to influence other people. They engage in behaviors which create the impression that they are competent and successful, thereby bolstering subordinate trust in decisions and increasing obedience in followers.

Charismatic leaders articulate ideological goals, describe future vision, set models of their behavior for followers to emulate and communicate high expectations about follower performance, while simultaneously expressing confidence in followers.[23]

## Leaders and Followers

As mentioned at the outset, leadership always involves a relationship between leader and follower. James MacGregor Burns has bemoaned the tendency in leadership research to separate followers from leaders, agreeing with the contention that leadership and followership always imply a reciprocal relationship.[24] Erickson asserts that great leaders "grow out of the extraordinary resonance they have with those whom they lead."[25] Group members bestow leadership on those individuals who structure experience in meaningful ways. These persons become leaders because they are able to frame experience in a way that provides a viable basis for action.

Twentieth century concepts of leader and follower relations seem to change over time from those which embody a uni-directional focus — either from leader to group or group to leader — to those which include both leaders and followers in a symbiotic relationship.

## Perception and Reality

Perception plays a large role in leader understanding. Individuals base their interpretation of information on their own, individual experience. This may be similar to, but never identical with, the experience of another person. The degree to which individual patterns overlap with those of others is the degree to which there is shared meaning among members of a group. It has been contended that if a group situation embodies strongly held competing definitions of reality, no clear pattern of leadership evolves.[26]

Even within groups where operational definitions of leadership seem to have been agreed upon, the question of who is or should be providing leadership may be observer-dependent and a product of selective perception, cognitive dissonance and other psychological factors.

On the other hand, who a group names as its leaders gives strong indication of that group's values at a moment in time. A society which, for instance, selects actors and sports heroes as its leaders reflects values or priorities different from a community which elevates philosophers and poets to leadership positions.

Americans tend to view leadership as positive. James MacGregor Burns has described the enormous hunger and yearning in modern society for creative leadership. Yet, Simonton asserts, "a leader can achieve a permanent place in history just as easily by being evil as by being good."[27]

## Monolithic or Pluralistic Leadership

The study of leadership in the social sciences has led to a major debate in both sociology and political science which centers on the character of the leadership structure within communities. Its participants argue about whether there is a power elite — a monopolistic and monolithic group of leaders with generalized ability to influence most affairs — or whether, on the other hand, leadership is situational to the decision at hand and is therefore factional, coalitional, and, to some degree, amorphous. The debate is both theoretical and empirical. How one stands on it, often determines how one will investigate leadership. Those who subscribe to the elite position use a reputational approach to identifying leaders. Those in the "pluralistic" camp are more prone to study specific cases and analyze collective decisions retrospectively.[28]

# Effective Leadership

In management literature, leadership is generally equated with "effective leadership." Some writers doubt that leaders are instrumental to how an organization succeeds,[29] while other commentators believe that leaders of an organization are of major significance in its success or failure.[30]

Leader effectiveness is thought of in terms of group indicators such as: performance, survival, growth, preparedness, capacity to deal with crises, attainment of goals. It is also measured in terms of subordinate satisfaction with the leader, subordinate commitment to group goals and the psychological well-being and development of group members.

Effective managers have been found to have "managerial motivation," which consists of a desire for power, a desire to compete with peers and a positive attitude toward authority figures. In addition, they exhibit socialized power orientation. That is, they focus energies not on personal aggrandizement or power for its own sake, but on dominance of the organization. They have a strong desire, therefore, for the group achievement of challenging goals and don't try to accomplish everything by themselves.

Effective managers bring three types of skills to bear on their work: human relations skills, technical skills, conceptual skills. They are persuasive, empathetic, reactive, analytic, good speakers and actors, and have good memories for detail.[31]

# Improving Leadership

If one assumes that leadership skills can be taught or developed, four areas have been found to show improvement in manager effectiveness after intervention and treatment.

> 1. **Selection.** Utilizing what knowledge has been gleaned from leadership studies, it is possible to select more appropriate people for positions. This can be achieved by analyzing the nature of the work to determine relevant skills and traits; by assessing candidates through tests, interviews and situational exercises to isolate particular traits and skills; by studying candidates' previous managerial history. In this way, the right person for the position can be identified.
> 2. **Training.** Teaching technical skills has been found relatively easy to accomplish. Conceptual skills can be developed through cases and games to learn problem analysis, forecasting,

planning, and decision-making. Creativity, too, can be enhanced. More difficult, however, is human-relations training, which to date has shown only small success.

3. **Situational Engineering.** Based on the situational context, studies have shown that rather than fit leaders to a situation, it may be preferable to alter the situation to improve its compatibility with available leaders. For instance, it might be desirable to increase or decrease a particular manager's authority or span of control.

4. **Organization Development and Leadership Improvement.** Intervention by specially trained change agents who measure the attitudes and perceptions of subordinates compared with those of managers to identify problems in communication, decision-making and interpersonal relations. Consultants may help with goal-setting, training sessions and team building.[32]

# Reading About Leadership

There is no shortage of information about leadership. Dozens of books on the subject are published each year. The papers contained in this volume make reference to a number of works on leadership. The four cited below are mentioned as points of departure for becoming acquainted with the topic of leadership.

In 1978, James MacGregor Burns published his monumental study of leadership in which he posited the importance of the "transformational" leader, who Burns considers the real mover and shaker in the world. Despite the fact that it has been around for a decade, the material does not seem dated and provides the best introduction to the subject of leadership.[33]

The second work is Warren Bennis and Burt Nanus' 1985 study which is called *Leaders: Strategies for Taking Charge.* Bennis, as mentioned above, belongs to the school which considers leadership skills teachable since each person is potentially a leader. Bennis and Nanus outline and describe four strategies pursued by true leaders. This book serves to extend leadership thinking into formal organizations rather than referring to the kind of societal leadership which is the focus of Burns' work.[34]

Barbara Kellerman's edited work, *Leadership: Multidisciplinary Perspectives,* includes essays by scholars from a variety of disciplines about leadership approaches within their own fields. The subjects included are history, psychoanalysis, political science, organizational behavior and feminist studies. Kellerman's work is particularly valuable in summarizing the traditional as well as radical approaches to the study of leadership.[35]

Finally, most students concur that *Stogdill's Handbook of Leadership* currently provides the most comprehensive description of leadership research. In it are descriptions of laboratory and field experiments testing all varieties of leadership hypotheses. The most recent edition, the second, was edited by Bernard Bass and was published in 1981.[36]

## Research into Library Leadership

Leadership until very recently was a much neglected subject in librarianship. *Library Literature* does not even utilize the term as an index heading. Those research efforts which treat leadership travel two distinct paths. One group of studies defines leadership within a management or administrative context. The other views leadership from an historical perspective, and in terms of the provision of one or many specific contributions to the profession.

Joanne Euster's recent study, parts of which are described in her paper, examines the perceived performance of academic library directors,[37] and Dragon's use of Fiedler's contingency model with public librarians[38] are two examples of recent library leadership studies in organizational contexts.

The other group of studies focuses on biography. Wiegand's investigation of Executive Board Members of the American Library Association from 1876 to 1917 presents a collective profile of library leaders along socio-economic lines and begins to apply historiometric procedures to study of library leadership.[39] My own research into leadership as a reflection of the social structure of the library field is a first step toward examining the question of the relationship between leadership and the agenda of a field.[40]

Indications of recent attention to the subject of "leadership" in the library field can be found in Herb White's *Library Journal* column, referred to by a number of the symposium's participants,[41] and to John Berry's assessment of new public library leaders in the same publication a few weeks earlier.[42] Another manifestation of the current interest is the publication of *Libraries in the 90s: What the Leaders Expect,* which identifies a number of library leaders and asks them to do a little crystal gazing.[43]

# In Conclusion

Whether trait or situation creates leadership; whether leaders are born or developed; whether leaders lead groups or merely function as the center of a nucleus; and whether leadership in communities is monolithic or pluralistic are all questions that students will continue to address — perhaps for centuries to come.

However, those who bemoan the "absence" of leadership are directing their complaints toward the wrong target. Leadership is an integral part of any social system and is, therefore, always present. The absence of shared group perceptions of who is providing leadership, however, may signal the absence of shared perceptions about aims and goals for the group, and therefore, the absence of a shared or common agenda. Leaders draw strength from their ability to articulate the common group goals and purposes. A group which does not share goals and purposes is hard pressed to share its perceptions of leadership

# Notes

1. Wildavsky, Aaron and Robert C. Tucker. *Politics as Leadership.* Columbia, Mo.: University of Missouri Press, 1981, p. 12.

2. Stogdill, Ralph M. *Stogdill's Handbook of Leadership,* revised and expanded by Bernard M. Bass. New York: The Free Press, 1981, p. 5.

3. Havelock, Ronald. *Planning for Innovation through Dissemination and Utilization of Knowledge.* Center for Research on Utilization of Scientific Knowledge. Ann Arbor, Mich.: University of Michigan, 1975, pp. 7–12.

4. Kellerman, Barbara, ed. *Leadership: Multidisciplinary Perspectives.* Englewood Cliffs, N.J.: Prentice-Hall, 1984, p. xi.

5. Yukl, Gary A. *Leadership in Organizations.* Englewood Cliffs, N.J.: Prentice-Hall, 1981, p. 3.

6. Stogdill. *Handbook of Leadership,* p. 7.

7. Burns, James MacGregor. *Leadership.* New York: Harper and Row, 1978, p. 2.

8. Gibb, Cecil A. "Leadership: Psychological Aspects" in *International Encyclopedia of the Social Sciences,* 1968, vol. 9.

9. Kellerman. *Leadership: Multidisciplinary Perspectives,* pp. ix–x.

10. Burns. *Leadership,* pp. 26–27.

11. One of the most interesting recent examples of this approach is Dean Keith Simonton's *Genius, Creativity and Leadership* (Cambridge: Harvard University Press, 1984), in which he looks at evidence from scientific studies and attempts to determine whether such forces as genes, family position, education, IQ and many other factors seem to characterize those identified as geniuses and leaders.

12. Crane, Diana. *Invisible Colleges: Diffusion of Knowledge in Scientific Communities.* Chicago: University of Chicago Press, 1972, p. 128.

13. Carlyle, Thomas. *On Heroes, Hero Worship, and the Heroic in History.* London. Oxford University Press, (1841) 1946.

14. Seligman, Lester G. "Leadership; Political Aspects" in *International Encyclopedia of the Social Sciences,* 1968, vol. 9.

15. Emerson, Ralph Waldo. "History." in *The Collected Works Ralph Waldo Emerson. Essays: First Series,* vol. II. Cambridge: Harvard University Press, 1979, p. 6.

16. Stogdill. *Handbook of Leadership,* pp. 75–82.

17. Filley, Alan C., Robert J. House and Steve Kerr. *Managerial Processes and Organization Behavior.* Glenview, Ill.: Scott, Foresman, 1976, pp. 241–242.

18. Fiedler, Fred E. *A Theory of Leadership Effectiveness.* New York: McGraw Hill, 1967, p. 6.

19. Bennis, Warren, and Burt Nanus. *Leaders: The Strategies for Taking Charge.* New York: Harper and Row, 1985.

20. Pigors, H.E., in Gibb. *International Encyclopedia of the Social Sciences,* vol. 9.

21. Weber, Max. *The Theory of Social and Economic Organization.* New York: Oxford University Press, 1947.

22. Hunt, Sonja. "The Role of Leadership in the Construction of Reality," in *Leadership: Multidisciplinary Perspectives,* edited by Barbara Kellerman. Englewood Cliffs, N.J.: Prentice-Hall, p. 161. An example of the new interest in charisma can be found in *The Spellbinders: Charismatic Political Leadership* by Ann Ruth Willner, New Haven: Yale University Press, 1984.

23. Yukl. *Leadership in Organizations,* pp. 59–62.

24. Burns. *Leadership,* p. 3.

25. Kellerman. *Leadership: Multidisciplinary Perspectives,* p. 74.

26. Smircich, Linda, and Gareth Morgan. "Leadership: Management of Meaning," *Journal of Applied Science,* 18:3, 1982.

27. Simonton. *Genius, Creativity and Leadership,* p. 27.

28. Representatives of the two postures are Hunter, Floyd, *Community Power Structure.* Chapel Hill: University of North Carolina Press, 1953, and Dahl, Robert, *Who Governs.* New Haven: Yale University Press, 1961.

29. Pfeffer, Jeffrey. "The ambiguity of leadership" in M.W. McCall, Jr., and M.M. Lombardo, *Leadership: Where Else Can We Go?* Durham, N.C.: Duke University Press, 1978.

30. Katz, Daniel, and Robert L. Kahn. *The Social Psychology of Organizations,* 2nd ed. New York: Wiley, 1978.

31. Yukl. *Leadership in Organizations,* pp. 38–65.

32. *Ibid.,* pp. 278–285.

33. Stogdill. *Handbook of Leadership.*

34. Burns. *Leadership.*

35. Bennis. *Leaders: The Strategies for Taking Charge.*

36. Kellerman. *Leadership: Multidisciplinary Perspectives.*

37. Euster, Joanne. *Activities and Effectiveness of the Academic Library Director.* Westport, Conn.: Greenwood Press, 1987.

38. Dragon, Andrea. "Leader Behavior in Changing Libraries in Charles McClure and A.R. Samuels, eds. *Strategies for Library Administration.* Libraries Unlimited, 1982.

39. Wiegand, Wayne. "ALA Executive Board Members, 1876–1917: A Collective Profile." *Libri,* 31:2, 1981.

40. Gertzog, Alice. *An Investigation into the Relationship between the Structure of Leadership and the Social Sturcture of the Library Profession.* Ph.D. Dissertation. New Brunswick, N.J. Rutgers University, 1989.

41. White, Herbert. "Oh, Where Have All the Leaders Gone?" *Library Journal.* 112 (16) Oct. 1, 1987.

42. Berry, John. "The New Library Directors." *Library Journal,* 112 (14) September 1, 1987.

43. Riggs, Donald, and Gordon Sabine, eds. *Libraries in the 90s; What the Leaders Expect.* Phoenix: Oryx Press, 1989.

# Leaders and Leadership:
# An Eclectic Bibliography

*Alice Gertzog*

The central problem in compiling a leadership bibliography is also the central problem in studying or researching leadership — the difficulty in defining the concept. This bibliography adopts an eclectic approach. Multiple orientations to understanding leadership appear in material drawn from multiple disciplines. Library-related books about leadership are interfiled with titles from other fields. Space considerations governed the decision to list only books (with the exception of one journal issue devoted entirely to the topic) despite the presence of much useful material in periodical articles, and in unpublished dissertations and papers.

The list is designed for both practitioners and scholars. Most of the titles cited have a research dimension, although a few more "popular" entries are included. The works themselves are primarily concerned with leadership in organizations. Several, however, deal with elective, societal or other specific kinds of leadership. Titles which treat such related concepts as "cognitive authority" (see, for instance, Patrick Wilson's *Second Hand Knowledge)*, intellectual leadership (Kadushin's *The American Intellectual Elite)* or leadership by expertise (Haskell's *The Authority of Experts*) are omitted.

Leadership bibliographies almost never duplicate each other. Names of a few authors may surface again and again — Bennis, Burns and Stogdill, for instance — but most lists contain entries which are chosen because they match the individual bibliographer's understanding of leadership.

There is no shortage of materials about leadership. Every day new titles appear on publishers' lists. Every management textbook contains at least one section or chapter about leaderhip. Generally, these texts provide a good entry point into the subject. The putative researcher would do well to look for instance, at Koontz & O'Donnell's *Principles of Management,* Wren's *The Evolution of Management Thought,* March's *Handbook of Organizations* and Katz and Kahn's *The Social Psychology of Organizations.* Library Science management textbooks also cover leadership, although generally in fewer pages (see, for instance, Stueart's *Library Management*). *The International Encyclopedia of the Social Sciences,* while dated, has three excellent introductory articles on leadership.

The 1980s experienced a breathtaking burst of popular management/leadership books based on "instant success" on the one hand and aspirations toward "excellence" on the other. Titles such as *The One-Minute Manager* spawned a host of books permitting readers to be *One-Minute Fathers* and *One-Minute Salespersons. In Search of Excellence* produced dozens of spin-off works which utilized the word "excellent" in their titles. Most of these books are omitted below.

The concept of leadership has only recently received interest and attention in the library field. *Library Literature* does not use it as a subject heading, and one must consult "Administration" for access to works relating to leadership. Most books and articles which have been written are either hortatory or cautionary, alternately bemoaning the absence of leadership or urging its development. In the past few years, however, there has been increasing attention to research into various aspects of library leadership, in formal organizations, within subfields and for librarianship as a whole.

Barber, James David. *Politics by Humans.* Duke University Press, 1988.
  A compilation of Barber's political writings on leadership, this volume illustrates and continues Barber's attempt to predict leader performance based on an analysis of leader personality. First suggested in his *Presidential Character,* Barber's well-known model utilizes two aspects of personality—level of activity and type of affect—to look at the interplay between character and style. Presidents are characterized as "active" or "passive" and as "positive" or "negative," providing a four-part typology. Barber's research places him solidly in the camp of those who find character to be the most important element in predicting leader behavior and effectiveness.
Bass, Bernard. *Leadership and Performance Beyond Expectations.* Free Press, 1985.
  An adherent of Burns' (see p. 75) concept of transformational

leadership, Bass explores the question of why certain leaders seem to motivate workers to far greater than anticipated productivity. Transactional leaders work with and through the group. The key is to turn transactional leaders into transformational ones, those who can actually change the environment and culture through leadership. Transformational leaders, in Bass' definition, are not far from charismatic ones and are to be found, in some measure, in all walks of life.

Bennis, Warren G., and Burt Nanus. *Leaders: The Strategies for Taking Charge*. Harper and Row, 1985.

Bennis is one of the best known and most admired of the management writers in the field of leadership theory and practice. He has written dozens of books and articles over the years, and has not hesitated to alter his opinions as circumstances and his understanding of them have changed. This work grew out of 90 interviews with business (60) and public sector (30) leaders to learn what they had in common. The authors found that the variety of managerial styles indicated little similar behavior. Managers did share, however, the way in which they provided vision to the organization and the way in which they were able to translate those visions into reality. The authors attack five traditional management myths: leadership is rare, leaders are born, leaders are charismatic, leadership exists only at an organization's top, and the leader controls, directs, prods and manipulates. A new book by Bennis, *Why Leaders Can't Lead: The Unconscious Conspiracy Continues,* was unavailable for examination when this manuscript went to press.

Blake, R.R., and J.S. Mouton. *The Managerial Grid III: The Key to Leadership Excellence*. Gulf, 1985.

A "Managerial Grid," which can be used to provide managers with feedback about their attitudes and behavior, is offered by Blake and Mouton. The grid utilizes as variables low and high orientations toward tasks and low and high amounts of concern for people in order to develop five managerial styles. The central, or fifth, style is one which represents a balanced concern for both task and people. Blake and Mouton contend that no single style is "best" in all situations. What is most effective depends on the people being managed and the situation in which the management occurs.

Burns, James MacGregor. *Leadership*. Harper and Row, 1978.

Though older than many of the other works in this bibliography, Burns' book is still required reading for the student of leadership. It is a fundamental statement on the nature and causes of leadership and utilizes and describes a wide range of psychological, sociological and political approaches. Burns makes a distinction between political leadership and the arbitrary exercise of power. The "true leader," Burns contends, develops a cooperative relationship with his followers. The tyrant, of course, does not. The leader can meet followers' needs either by helping them to achieve the goals they already desire or by bringing about a moral advance that enables them to recognize imperatives of which they were not aware. The former type of leadership Burns terms "transactional," and the latter, "transformational."

Cleveland, Harlan. *The Knowledge Executive*. Truman Talley Books/ Dutton, 1985.

Profound questions about the roles of specialists and those of generalists in significant decision-making situations are raised by Cleveland. He builds on the premise that more than half of all work now done in the United States is information work. Because the manner in which information is produced and disseminated differs fundamentally from the way in which tangible goods are produced and distributed, a type of leadership that is more participatory, more concerned with consensus is required. Effective leadership, therefore, will be provided by the generalist rather than the specialist, contends Cleveland, because no one person can know enough about the technical aspects of what is going on to supervise properly an entire operation.

Dumont, Rosemary R., ed. "Women and Leadership in the Library Profession." *Library Trends* 34: 169–353. Fall, 1985.

A wide-ranging compilation of articles about the position of women in the higher echelons of library management. Includes, in addition to an extensive bibliographic essay, an historical assessment of the changing role of women in libraries, consideration of the motivation of women to manage, a review of career development patterns by gender, and suggested correctives to the current male-female imbalance in library leadership positions.

Euster, Joanne R. *The Academic Library Director: Management Activities and Effectiveness*. Greenwood, 1988.

One of the first full-blown empirical studies of library leadership. Euster employs both organizational and open systems theory to look at varying styles of leadership activity, reputation effectiveness and management of change exhibited by directors of research libraries. She surveys the perceptions of those in the environment external to the library — university administrators — and middle management subordinates in the library itself about library directors. These she compares with how directors perceive themselves. From her findings she develops an eight-part typology to describe leadership types.

Fiedler, Fred. *A Theory of Leadership Effectiveness.* McGraw-Hill, 1967.

Developer of the contingency theory, Fiedler maintains that leader effectiveness is not only a function of the leader's style, but is dependent on the relationship between the leader's style, the degree of structure in the task, the amount of authority he or she has, and the degree to which there is subordinate acceptance of the leader. No single trait, therefore, will predict leader effectiveness. Fielder's seminal model produced ambiguous results, but it continues to generate interest and new experimentation.

Gardner, John. *Excellence: Can We Be Equal and Excellent Too?* Rev. ed. Norton, 1987.

Gardner questions whether there can be peaceful coexistence of equality and excellence in this plea for the development of leadership in the society. We love the idea, he says, of free and fair competition, while recognizing that it produces mixed results. Equality may foster great achievements and release human energy. It may also allow exploiters and abusers of power to develop. Democracy permits us to control the negative elements, but it also has the potential to inhibit excellence and stifle the person of superior gifts. The challenge, Gardner asserts, is to provide opportunities and rewards so that individuals at every level can achieve their full potential, perform at their best and harbor no resentment toward those at any other level.

Georgi, Charlotte, and Robert Bellanti, eds. *Excellence in Library Management.* Haworth, 1985. [also published as *Journal of Library Administration* 6 no. 3, Fall 1985.]

Proceedings of the tenth "Management for Librarians Workshop," which focused on "excellent" libraries. Two special librarians, two public librarians and two academic librarians describe the qualities which permit their institutions to claim that accolade. Few of the writers identify or point to the same factors to explain "excellence." A final essay by management expert John McDonough focuses on competition, power and politics, as well as on the irrational side of an organization.

Keegan, John. *The Mask of Command.* Viking, 1988.

Leadership, Keegan contends, is a political activity. The leader fashions a "mask" to make himself or herself identifiable to followers in a form that they want or need. "Masks" are not at odds with the personality of their wearers, but neither are they simply a reflection of their owners' personalities. The masks worn by leaders are based on a political assessment about followers and the situation being faced. While Keegan, an historian, draws on military leadership and focuses on commanders, his theories are not less germane to managers. Leaders, he says, share an identity with their followers based on a common experience, and leadership always describes a relationship.

Kellerman, Barbara, ed. *Leadership: Multidisciplinary Perspectives.* Prentice-Hall, 1984.

A series of essays on leadership from the perspectives of history, sociology, political science, philosophy, anthropology and psychology, with an incisive introduction by James MacGregor Burns. The volume shows the diversity in type, nature, and direction of leadership studies as well as the diverse conceptualizations each of those disciplines brings to the subject.

Kotter, John P. *The Leadership Factor.* Free Press, 1988.

A treatment of leadership needs and behavior at all managerial levels of the corporation. Kotter designates articulating a vision of the future, strategy formulation, network building and motivating key people as essential leadership activities. Utilizing these elements, he discusses effective leadership, leadership failures and the problems which they incur, and ways to improve the quality of leadership. The extensive questionnaire instrument/interview schedule utilized to provide data is included.

Loden, Marilyn. *Feminine Leadership, or, How to Succeed in Business Without Being One of the Boys.* Times Books, 1986.

One of a spate of women-oriented management books that have appeared since the later 1970s. Loden, while depending both on research and the works of feminist Carol Gilligan, plays a risky game of asserting that organizations need the particular traits women can offer. Among these are intuition, sensitivity to the needs of others and greater capacity for work under stress. Interviews with 200 corporate women convinces Loden that women possess a stronger work ethic and work harder than their male counterparts. For a more scholarly, theory-based assessment of corporate treatment of women, see Rosabeth Kanter's *Men and Women of the Corporation.*

Maccoby, Michael. *The Gamesman*. Simon & Schuster, 1976.

Based on interviews with corporate leaders, Maccoby develops a four-part typology which includes "craftsmen" who produce high-quality finished products; "company men," concerned more with security than success; "jungle fighters," whose goal is power and is evidenced in their roles either as lions (conquerors) or foxes (stealthy nest builders) and finally "Gamesmen," those mainly interested in competition and challenge. The personalities of Gamesmen are well suited to the modern corporation, which is similarly oriented toward competition, as well as toward innovation, interdependent teams and fast-moving flexibility.

_____. *The Leader*. Simon & Schuster, 1981.

Here Maccoby concentrates on six leaders who share such basic personality traits as intelligence, ambition, will and optimism. Although there are differences between them, all possess the three qualities which Maccoby claims as most significant for developing successful leadership: a caring, respectful attitude; flexibility about people and about organizational structure; and a participative approach to management. Maccoby warns that power must be exercised efficiently and wisely and that the leader must present a model that others will want to emulate.

Mintzberg, H. *The Nature of Managerial Work*. Harper and Row, 1973.

One of the early studies to look at what managers actually do. Mintzberg used a diary approach to systematically research how managers spend their time. From this he developed ten managerial roles, which he grouped into three categories. Although one role is specifically designated as "leader," Mintzberg asserts that leadership permeates all of a manager's activities. He found that the manager is driven to brevity, fragmentation and superficiality in his tasks. Useful for the methodology, as well as for the findings.

Peters, Thomas. *Thriving on Chaos: Handbook for a Management Revolution*. Knopf, 1987.

More broadly based than *In Search of Excellence* (see below), here Peters suggests a host of approaches to help U.S. corporations who have been swept up in chaotic change. The solutions, which he offers with messianic fervor, include the need for innovation; empowering the organization's staff; and developing change-oriented leadership and sensitive managers.

_____, and Robert Waterman, Jr. *In Search of Excellence: Lessons from America's Best-Run Companies*. Harper and Row, 1982.

The first of the popular management books which concentrated on "excellence." The authors studied how 62 "excellent" American companies attained and maintained their status. They found eight characteristics common to all of them, as well as the fact that each had been "blessed with unusual leadership especially in the early days of the company." Among the eight prescriptions for success: have a bias for action, produce *through* people and stay close to the business.

Riggs, Donald., ed. *Library Leadership: Visualizing the Future.* Oryx, 1982.

A series of articles by well-known library field members predicting future leadership problems within both structural and functional segments of the library profession. For instance, there are pieces dealing with small and large public libraries, school library media programs community colleges and special libraries, as well as articles which consider the future of technical services, collection development and reference. The book assumes that an adequate analysis of leadership involves a study not only of leaders, but also of situations in which they must function.

_____, and G. Sabine. *Libraries in the 90's: Viewpoints of Leaders.* Oryx, 1988.

Riggs and Sabine interviewed 25 leaders, representing various types of libraries and library-connected institutions, to learn what they think the future holds. Arranged topically, one section speaks directly about leadership, another looks at dream libraries. In view of the importance of leaders to the agenda-setting process, their prognostications are of interest and may, to some extent, be self-fulfilling. Biographical profiles of the 25 leaders are included.

Sayles, L.R. *Leadership: What Effective Managers Really Do ... and How They Do It.* McGraw-Hill, 1979.

Rather than study a single management skill, Sayles emphasizes the behavioral inter-relationships and principles of the management process. The management function is seen as a synthesis of skills which are applied "artistically," not only as scientific problem-solving. Sayles delineates leadership roles such as communication, power, charisma and reconciliation.

Schein, Edgar. *Organization Culture and Leadership.* Jossey-Bass, 1985.

Leadership is critical both to the formation of an organization's culture and to that organization's cultural change, contends Schein. In addition, leadership and culture management are central to understanding organizations. An organization's culture, he maintains, develops around the external and internal problems that groups face and gradually becomes abstracted into general and basic assumptions about the nature of reality, the world and the place of the group within it on the one hand and the character of time, space, human nature, human activity and human relationships, on the other.

Simonton, D.K. *Genius, Creativity & Leadership; Historiometric Inquiries.* Harvard University Press, 1984.

Simonton uses quantitative methods to test nomothetic hypotheses based on data bases constructed from historical populations. He applies cliometric and psychometric techniques to learn whether there are significant relationships between, say, artistic or revolutionary activity and birth order; whether age can be correlated with achievement, and, if so, in what endeavors. The findings are questionable and bear further investigation. The methodology, however, holds promise for use in other leadership studies. In the library field, Wiegand's study of Executive Board members of the American Library Association from 1876 to 1917 uses quantitative methods to develop a collective profile of the group along socio-economic lines (included in his *Politics of an Emerging Profession*).

Stogdill, Ralph M. *Stogdill's Handbook of Leadership; A Survey of Theory and Research.* Revised and expanded by Bernard Bass. Free Press, 1981.

The most comprehensive listing and report of leadership research which includes consideration of leadership. A mandatory first source for leadership researchers. Among the topics receiving attention are leadership definition and theory, personality, situation, power and legitimacy, leader-follower interaction and leadership styles. In addition, there are sections devoted to leadership and ethnic and racial minorities, as well as to leadership and women. A 1981 publication date limits the book's usefulness.

Tucker, Robert. *Politics as Leadership.* University of Missouri Press, 1981.

Politics, says Tucker, is essentially leadership of a political community rather than only an exercise of power. He embraces the controversial position that leaders control the course of events and flourish in difficult times. The leader's task is to influence or manipulate the minds and actions of followers in order to mobilize forces to control events.

Vroom, V.H., and P.W. Yetton. *Leadership and Decision Making.* University of Pittsburgh Press, 1973.

The authors have developed a diagnostic tool to enable leaders to choose the managerial style which will work best in a given situation. Seven rules are applied to the characteristics of a problem through use of a decision tree. Twenty-three problem situations, each with a feasible set of decision processes appropriate to solve the problem, emerge. By following the tree, managers can determine the appropriate form and amount of participation in decision-making by subordinates in different classes of situations.

Willner, Ann Ruth. *The Spellbinders.* Yale University Press, 1984.

An example of the increased attention paid to charismatic leadership in recent years and to the importance attributed to it. Willner clarifies the concept of charisma, analyzes its components and examines how it is exemplified by a number of selected leaders. She offers the following four generalizations about the behavior of charismatic leaders: an assimilation to one or more of the culture's dominant myths, the performance of heroic feats, the projection of a powerful aura, and outstanding rhetorical abilities.

Woodsworth, Anne, and Barbara von Wahlde, eds. *Leadership for Research Libraries; A Festschrift for Robert M. Hayes.* Scarecrow, 1988.

In this first-rate volume, a group of directors of major academic libraries attempts to stimulate more thought and research effort about leadership for research libraries. Each of the eleven original articles tackles a different aspect of research library leadership by presenting the current thinking, summarizing available studies and pointing out research gaps. Following a literature review, there are pieces on the campus context, the library organization, leadership development, the role of library schools and career management, among others.

Yukl, Gary. *Leadership in Organizations.* Prentice-Hall, 1981.

Summarizes recent behavioral research about managerial leadership to explain a model of action for effective leadership. Included in Yukl's model are reciprocal influence processes, power, leader effectiveness and personal and situational theories wich he draws together in an integrated framework. Yukl contends that more has been learned about leadership than most experts acknowledge.

# About the Contributors

JOANNE EUSTER currently serves as university librarian at Rutgers, a position she has held since 1986. Previously, she was library director at San Francisco State University. Her education includes an MLS and an MBA from the University of Washington and a Ph.D. from the University of California–Berkeley. Her doctoral dissertation won the Association for Library and Information Science's award in 1987. She is the author of *The Academic Library Director: Management Activities and Effectiveness* (Greenwood Press, 1987) and numerous articles. Professionally active, she served as President of the Association of College and Research Libraries for 1987-88.

ALICE GERTZOG has taught Management and Collection Development at SCILS, Rutgers University, where she also served as acting director of Professional Development Studies. Prior to coming to Rutgers, she was director of the Meadville (PA) Public Library. She received an MLS from Catholic University and a Ph.D. from Rutgers University.

EMILY MOBLEY has been the associate director of Purdue University Libraries since 1986. Her prior position was library director, GMI Engineering and Management Institute. She holds BA and MLS degrees from the University of Michigan where she is a Ph.D. candidate. Currently she is president of the Special Libraries Association. Among her publications is *Special Libraries at Work* (Shoe String Press, 1984) which she coauthored with Elizabeth Ferguson.

JANA VARLEJS is director of Professional Development Studies and associate professor at Rutgers University. She received her MLS from Rutgers University and is a Ph.D. candidate at the University of Wisconsin–Madison. The author of numerous library publications, she has served as faculty liaison to the alumni, is instrumental in the alumni-faculty symposia and has edited five of the proceedings.

ROBERT WEDGEWORTH is dean of the School of Library Service, Columbia University. He came to this position from the executive directorship of the American Library Association, an office he held from 1972 to 1985. Educated at Wabash College, he holds an MLS from the University of Illinois and has pursued further graduate studies at Washington University,

123579

St. Louis, and at Rutgers University. Among his numerous activities, he serves as a member of the Executive Board of the International Federation of Library Organizations, is on the Advisory Council for the Library of Congress Center for The Book, on the board of directors of the Public Service Satellite Consortium and a member of the board of trustees of the Newberry Library in Chicago. He has been the editor of the ALA *Yearbook of Library and Information Services* as well as of the ALA *World Encyclopedia of Library and Information Services.*